THE SECRET TO GETTING YOUR K-1(FIANCÉ) VISA APPROVED

(Step by step guide with legal tips)

CONTENTS

DEDICATION

Dedicate the book to my Mother and Father, who were also successful K-1 Applicants.

AUTHOR BIO

Mr. Shaw worked at the University of North Dakota (UND) Immigration Law Clinic, where he practised extensive immigration law as a Student Attorney. At the UND Immigration Law Clinic, Mr. Shaw advocated heavily for his clients regarding asylum cases, employment/work authorizations, Temporary Protected Status (TPS), Immigration Visas, Immigration Green Cards and other clients specific Immigration legal matters. Mr. Shaw has also successfully provided guidance and legal advice on the laws of Marriage-Based Green Cards, Fiancé Visas (K-1), Naturalization/Citizenship, Adjustment of Status (AOS) and Family-Based Immigration Petitions, particularly for Immediate Relatives.

After law school, Mr. Shaw worked at a premier Hollywood, top-ranking boutique and SAG-AFTRA Franchised entertainment Talent Agency firm. There, Mr. Shaw was exposed to the intrinsic value of the entertainment business and the immigration side of it. Mr Shaw was exposed to Individuals with Extraordinary Ability or Achievements (O-1 Visas), Business/Tourist Visas (B-1 & B-2 Visas), Immigration Student Visas (F-1 Visas), Optional Practical Training Benefits (OPT), Work Authorization, Advance Parole (Travel Permission), Green Cards and plenty more, all pertaining to the entertainers within and outside of the talent agency firm. Mr. Shaw is proud to succeed in assisting several clients within and outside of the talent agency, acquiring their O-1 visas and renewals of the O-1 visa, OPTs, work authorization, Business/Tourist visas and Green Cards. Mr. Shaw continues to maintain strong relationships in the entertainment industry and advises Talent Agents and others as it pertains to Immigration law.

Mr. Shaw is the proud founder of Shaw 3 Law Firm (S3LF) and a licensed California Attorney licensed to practise Immigration Law in all 50 States. He received his B.A. degree from the University of California of Riverside and his law degree from the University of North Dakota School of Law. He is also admitted and part of the country's largest and most prestigious Immigration Lawyers Association (American Immigration Lawyers Association (AILA). This enables Mr. Shaw to deliver higher quality Immigration legal services throughout the country.

Mr. Shaw also provides his clients with an additional service for those interested in investing or purchasing real estate and/or acquiring a residential mortgage in the state of California. He understands that clients can shy away from lucrative real estate opportunities, particularly with their pending or completed immigration matters. He alleviates their problem by assisting them and providing them with a sense of ease throughout their real estate process from acquiring a mortgage to homeownership or investments. Mr. Shaw states, "Helping clients out with their immigration matter is rewarding, but helping clients out pursue their American Dream of homeownership or real estate investments are even more rewarding." Mr. Shaw is a California licensed Real Estate Broker and Mortgage Loan Broker.

Mr. Shaw's primary goal is to build his reputation to be a top and premier Immigration Lawyer and Law Firm in the United States while all at the same time assisting his clients in accomplishing their Immigration goals. He understands the ever-changing, complex, and dynamic field of Immigration Law, including its implications in Criminal Law, Family Law, and Business law. He also focuses acutely on government agencies' actions and keeps up to date on the latest policies, rule changes, and changes in the law such as: the U.S. Citizenship and Immigration Services (USCIS); The United States Department of Homeland Security (DHS); U.S Immigration and Customs (ICE); U.S Customs and Border Protection (CBP); Department of Labor (DOL); and Department of Justice (DOJ). Mr Shaw and his team ensure to work with clients to ensure that government forms are completed correctly so that his clients' cases are processed quickly and efficiently. Mr Shaw dedicates his work and passion in Immigration law to work on each case in a collaborative, team approach to keep abreast with the demands and needs of local U.S clients as well as clients nationwide.

Mr. Shaw enjoys hiking, playing outdoor sports, and riding his motorcycle. He is mixed with Indonesian and is deeply ingrained in his Indonesian culture. He also speaks Bahasa Indonesia.

CREDENTIAL SECTION

EDUCATION:

6

University of North Dakota School of Law, J.D. (2017)

University of California Riverside, B.A., Political Science Law & Society (2014)

CURRENT RELEVANT LICENSES:

California Talent Agent License (Lic #TA152823)

California Attorney State Bar License (Lic #330934), also licensed to practice Immigration Law in all 50 states.

California Real Estate Broker License (Lic #01890821)

California Mortgage Loan Broker License (Lic #1580013)

PROFESSIONAL ASSOCIATIONS:

American Immigration Lawyers Association (AILA)

FOR MORE INFORMATION, CONSULTANT, AND LEGAL ADVICE, VISIT

Shaw 3 Law Firm *@ www.shaw3lawfirm.com*

INTRODUCTION

What is the K1 Visa?

The K1 visa (also called the fiancé visa) is a special visa that allows the fiancé of a U.S. citizen to enter the United States, marry their U.S. citizen fiancé, and adjust their status in the United States to get their green card.

To get a K1 visa, your U.S. citizen fiancé must file a Form I-129f on your behalf in addition to other steps discussed below. Your U.S. citizen fiancé is the petitioner (person filing the petition) and you (the person getting the K1 visa) is the beneficiary (person benefiting from the petition).

Getting a K1 visa based on your engagement as a U.S. citizen can be complicated. You must meet specific eligibility requirements and you must follow precise steps. If you fail to file paperwork correctly or complete the necessary steps, your case may face huge delays or, even worse, be denied.

Regarding the K1 visa processing time, it takes about eight months to 1 year to get your K1 visa. Once you are in the United States on your K1 visa, it takes about another 7 to 9 months to get your green card and become a legal permanent resident.

PETITION

To establish K-1 visa classification for an alien fiancée, an American citizen must file a petition, Form I-129F, Petition for Fiancée, with the United States Citizenship and Immigration

8

Services (USCIS) Office having jurisdiction over the place of the petitioner's residence in the United States.

Such petitions may not be adjudicated abroad.

USCIS will forward the approved petition to the National Visa Center (NVC). The (NVC) will do a background check, and then your case will be forwarded to the respective U.S embassry or consulate. At this point, the foreign fiancé may proceed with the K1 visa application (DS-160) and medical exam. The embassy will then schedule an interview soon.

A petition is usually valid for a period of at or around four months from the date of USCIS action and may be revalidated by the consular officer.

INELIGIBILITY/WAIVER

Applicants who have an infectious disease or have a dangerous physical or mental disorder; are drug addicts; have committed serious criminal acts, including crimes involving moral turpitude, drug trafficking, and prostitution; are likely to become a public charge; have used fraud or other illegal means to enter the United States, or can become ineligible for a visa, let alone permanent residency, thus may be refused a visa.

It is important to contact an Immigration Attorney for more information on this.

APPLYING FOR A FIANCE VISA

Before the foreign fiancé may apply for the K-1 visa, the U.S citizen must file a petition that establishes a qualifying relationship. To begin the process the U.S citizen will file an I-129F petition package to the (USCIS) with necessary documentations.

This will usually include the the following documents:

- ✓ A copy of a valid passport of the petitioner & beneficairy
- ✓ A copy of the Birth certificate of the petitioner & beneficiary
- ✓ A copy of Divorce or death certificate(s) of any previous spouse(s)
- ✓ Proof of intent to marry. A simple statement from the petitioner & benefiairy will usually suffice
- ✓ Police records if petitioner has ever been involved in any crimes
- ✓ Passport style photograph of petitioner & beneficiary
- ✓ Evidence of valid relationship with Photographs
- ✓ Legal documents of any name change
- ✓ USCIS Filing Fee

U.S. PORT OF ENTRY

Upon the benefiairy arrival in the United States, the marriage must take place within 90 days of admission into the United States.

Following the marriage, the alien spouse must apply to the USCIS to establish a record of entry for conditional permanent residence status.

After two years, the alien fiancé may apply to the USCIS for removal of the conditional status.

ADDITIONAL INFORMATION

Family Members

10

The unmarried, minor children of a K-1 beneficiary derive "K-2" nonimmigrant visa status from the parent so long as the children are named in the petition.

A separate petition is not required if the children accompany or follow the alien fiancée within one year from the date of issuance of the K-1visa.

Thereafter, a separate immigrant visa petition is required.

K-1 FIANCÉ VISA OVERVIEW

Terminology:

Fiancé - The term fiancé will be used to include both male and female prospective spouses USCIS – the United States Citizenship and Immigration Services

Petitioner - The U.S. citizen who files a petition with a USCIS office in the United States on behalf of a fiancé asking that he or she be admitted to the United States for the purpose of marriage

Petition - USCIS form I-129 (F) "Petition to Classify Status of Alien Fiancé or Fiancé for Issuance of Nonimmigrant Visa."

Beneficiary - The fiancé named in the petition

K-1 Visa - The visa category for the fiancé of a U.S. citizen

K-2 Visa - The visa category for the minor children of a K-1 visa holder

Packet 3 - Information that the Embassy sends to your fiancé, which specifies the documents that must be obtained and presented at the visa interview

Packet 4 - Information that the Embassy sends to your fiancé setting an appointment date and explaining how to obtain the required medical examination

First Step -- Filing the Petition

To begin the K-1 process, you file a petition at the United States Citizenship and Immigration Services (USCIS) office having jurisdiction over your current or intended residence in the U.S.

There is a current filing fee of $535 for the I-129F petition. This is a check or money order made out to U.S. Department of Homeland Security. The filing fee is subject to change, so it is important to always verify the filing fee for I-129F petition.

The children of your fiancé must be listed in the petition even if they will not be traveling at this time.

You must present the following supporting documentation with your petition:

- ✓ A copy of a valid passport of the petitioner & beneficairy
- ✓ A copy of the Birth certificate of the petitioner & beneficiary
- ✓ A copy of Divorce or death certificate(s) of any previous spouse(s)
- ✓ Proof of intent to marry. A simple statement from the petitioner & benefiairy will usually suffice
- ✓ Police records if petitioner has ever been involved in any crimes
- ✓ Passport style photograph of petitioner & beneficiary
- ✓ Evidence of valid relationship with Photographs
- ✓ Legal documents of any name change
- ✓ USCIS Filing Fee (currently $535).

After you have collected the documentation and completed the I-129F petition, then you will usually need to file it to a USCIS lockbox in Dallas. Check the USCIS website at www.uscis.gov/i-129f to get the appropirate address.

Usually within a few weeks after filing the petition, your fiancé should get back written confirmation that the papers are being processed, together with a receipt for the fees. This notice (on Form I-797C) will also contain your immigration file number, which is useful if the decision gets delayed.

Ask the USCIS directly if you have further questions about the petition process and petition approval requirements. You may contact the USCIS at 1-800-375-5283. Or you can contact an Immigration Attorney.

Second Step -- When Your Petition is Approved

When you receive the approval notice from USCIS, USCIS will send a Form I-797 Notice of Action to your U.S. citizen fiancé, indicating the approval. At the same time, USCIS will send a copy of your file to an office called the National Visa Center (NVC), which will assign you a case number and transfer the file to the appropriate U.S consulate in your country.

Your petition is usually valid for four months but can be extended by making a request to the Embassy if a visa cannot be issued during that period and the intention to marry still exists. You simply must contact the Consulate and request an extension.

Third Step – NVC to Consular Processing

If your fiancé security check comes back clean, your approved K1 visa petition will be routed to the Bureau of Consular Affairs. The Bureau of Consular Affairs will send your file to

14

the U.S Embassy in your fiancé country. Usually at this stage, the fiancé will start filling out and submit Form DS-160 online at the Consular Electronic Application Center website, https://ceac.state.gov/genniv. Please note that even though your spouse did not have to file a separate I-129F petition for any children, you will usually need to file a separate DS-160 for each of them to get a K2 visa.

After receiving your visa petition, the U.S Embassy (usually in the country of origin) sends the fiancé a letter with instructions for scheduling the medical exam and interview. The petitioner (U.S. citizen) usually does not attend the embassy interview.

Each U.S Embassy or consular post has different procedures, so listen only to what your consulate tells you to do.

Usually in this letter provided by the U.S. Embassy the fiancé will need to bring to the interview at least the following items:

- ✓ Completed Copy of Form DS-160, Online Nonimmigrant Visa Application and Confirmation Page.
- ✓ Any and all originals of documents submitted in connection with the visa petition, such as U.S petitioner's birth certificate and proof of any previous marriages were legally ended
- ✓ Fiancé passport valid for at least six months beyond the intended period of stay in the U.S.
- ✓ Police Certificates from your present country of residence and all countires where you have lived for six months or more since age 16
- ✓ Results of Medical Examination, in an unopended envelope

- ✓ Completed Form I-134, Affidavit of Support with supporting documentation such as proof of U.S. citizen's employment, copy of U.S. citizen's most recent federal tax returns, and letter from U.S. citizen's bank(s) confirming the account
- ✓ Fiancé original birth certificate
- ✓ Passport-Style Photos (2)
- ✓ Evidence of any previous marriages have been terminated
- ✓ Evidence of bona fide relationship with the U.S. citizen petitioner
- ✓ Visa Fees, which is also called the "machine readable visa" (MRV) fee – (currently $265) online
- ✓ Any other documents specifically requested

Make sure you make mulitiple copies of each of the above. One for yourself, one for the interview and one to keep at home.

Fourth Step -- Scheduling an interview

The Embassy will send out a Packet explaining the process of obtaining medical exams and scheduling an appointment for a visa interview. Again, the U.S Embassy (usually in the country of origin) sends the fiancé a letter with instructions for scheduling the medical exam and interview. The petitioner (U.S. citizen) usually does not attend the embassy interview. The U.S. Embassy will instruct the Fiancé to return some of the documents immediately. Other documents will be kept until the interview.

Fifth Step -- The Visa Interview

On the date of the appointment your fiancé should go to the Immigrant Visa Section of the Embassy.

Minor children under 14 part of the petition usually do not need to attend the interview. But it is always important to bring them.

Your fiancé, if have not already, may need to fill out a Nonimmigrant Visa Application (DS-160) in duplicate.

Each dependent child will also need Nonimmigrant Visa Applications in duplicate. Original documents, not copies, should be brought to the interview.

Originals of primary documents, such as birth, marriage, and death records, will be returned to the applicant after the interview.

The fiancé will likely be asked to present:

- ✓ Completed Copy of Form DS-160, Online Nonimmigrant Visa Application and Confirmation Page.
- ✓ Any and all originals of documents submitted in connection with the visa petition, such as U.S petitioner's birth certificate and proof of any previous marriages were legally ended
- ✓ Fiancé passport valid for at least six months beyond the intended period of stay in the U.S.
- ✓ Police Certificates from your present country of residence and all countires where you have lived for six months or more since age 16
- ✓ Medical exam results for the beneficiary and any dependent children

17

- ✓ Completed Form I-134, Affidavit of Support with supporting documentation such as proof of U.S. citizen's employment, copy of U.S. citizen's most recent federal tax returns, and letter from U.S. citizen's bank(s) confirming the account
- ✓ Fiancé original birth certificate
- ✓ Passport-Style Photos (2)
- ✓ Evidence of any previous marriages have been terminated
- ✓ Evidence of bona fide relationship with the U.S. citizen petitioner. This documentation is the pictures together, emails, letters, engagement ring receipt, relationship letter, etc.
- ✓ Visa Fees, which is also called the "machine readable visa" (MRV) fee – (currently $265) online
- ✓ Valid passports for the beneficiary and any dependent children Birth certificates for the beneficiary and any dependent children
- ✓ Any other documents specifically requested

After a consular officer has reviewed the case, the fiancé will be interviewed.The consular officer will likely ask your fiancé questions about your relationship, such as how you met and when you decided to marry. The consular officer is required by law to verify that your relationship with your fiancé is real and that you do intend to marry within 90 days of your fiancé's arrival in the United States.

Provided everything is in order at the time of the interview, your fiancé may receive a visa the same day. And if you have not already, the fiancé and each dependent child will pay a non- refundable machine-readable-visa (MRV)- currently ($265) fee on the day of the interview. For citizens of countries that charge an extra fee to U.S. citizens seeking to go there, there may also be an additional fee the fiancé may pay called a "reciporcity fee."

Thereafter, supporting documentation, including the K petition, birth certificate, Nonimmigrant Visa Application, and medical exam will be placed in a sealed envelope and given to the applicant for presentation to U.S Customs and Boarder Protection (CBP) at the port of entry for the fiancé to present at the Point of Entry into the United States.

STEP-BY-STEP INSTRUCTIONS

1. U.S. Citizen completes and signs the following forms:

- Form I-129F – Petition for Alien Fiancé.
- I-134 – Affidavit of Support.

2. U.S. Citizen writes a check or money order for $535 (current fee) to: "U.S. Department of Homeland Security".

3. U.S. Citizen gathers the necessary documents in the Required Supporting Document Checklist. Do not send original documentation of items you cannot easily replace (e.g. passport, birth certificate, etc.) A clear photocopy is sufficient. It is not necessary to have the copies notarized.

4. U.S. Citizen sends the following to the appropriate USCIS Regional Service Center:

•Form I-129F.

•Copies of all Supporting Documents.

•Check for $535 (current fee) to "U.S. Department of Homeland Security" for Form I-129F. (Staple the check to the I-129F)

5. U.S. Citizen sends the following to Fiancé.

•Original Form I-134 Affidavit of Support

•Copies of Proof of Financial Support from Required Document Checklist

6. VERY IMPORTANT: Make a copy of each Form and document you send to the USCIS for your own records.

7. U.S. citizen sends the application, supporting documents and fee to the appropriate USCIS Regional Service Center. Send the package Certified Return Receipt via the U.S. Postal Service or via a commercial service, such as Federal Express. Make sure to get a receipt with a tracking number.

8. You will receive a Form I-797, Notice of Receipt from the USCIS, usually within three weeks after sending in the application package. This Form will tell you that the USCIS has received your application and that it is in the cue to be processed. It will also give you a case number and a telephone number of an automated system to call to check the status of your application. The number is usually busy during business hours, so you may have to call in the evening to get through.

9. Next, you should receive an approval notice from the USCIS.

10. Make a copy of the approval notice for your records.

11. Send the original approval notice, along with a copy of each Form and document you filed with the USCIS, to your fiancé.

12. Your fiancé should receive a Packet from the American Consulate. The Packet is essentially a checklist that is to be

completed, signed and returned to the American Consulate. If your fiancé does not receive the Packet in 4 weeks, he or she may go to the American Consulate in person with the approval notice to request the Packet .

13. The American Consulate will then issue another Packet: a packet of forms to complete and documents to obtain (see required document checklist, bottom portion). They will also schedule an interview date.

14. Your fiancé is to complete the forms in the packet and gather the documents requested before the interview date.

15. At the interview, your fiancé is to present the completed forms, the requested documents, the approval notice and the copy of the file that you sent. The Consulate Officer will review the documents, ask a few questions (see interview questions), and issue fiancé the K-1Visa in his/her passport. Your fiancé's children will receive the K-2 Visa in their passports.

How the USCIS determines which Applications it Accepts and Rejects

The USCIS offices are overworked and understaffed. The applications that are approved the quickest usually have the following characteristics:

1)The applications are typed whenever possible.

2)The Supporting documents are organized. Use paper clips and binder clips to separate documents.

3)More documentation is better than less. More letters, more phone bills, etc.

4)Send Return Receipt Requested via U.S Postal Mail or via a Commercial Overnight Service (FedEx, etc.)

If your application package is well organized and complete, you will more likely than not receive a quicker approval. If your application package is not well organized and complete, it will take the USCIS worker longer to sort through your application and determine if it is complete or not.

THE APPLICATION PROCESS

Step 1: Gathering the Required Supporting Documents

The first step to undertake is to gather the required supporting documents to be sent with the United States Citizenship and Immigration Services (USCIS) forms to the USCIS.

Keep in mind that there are a few items you will need from your fiancé, so it is wise to start the gathering process as early as possible.

Note that all documents in a foreign language must be accompanied by a notarized English translation. These documents (birth certificate, divorce decree, etc.) may be translated either in your fiancé's native country or in the U.S.

Required Document Checklist – K-1 Fiancé Visa

Step 1: Required Documents & Forms for the K-1 Fiancé Visa:

(Please make sure these are all enclosed in the package you send to the USCIS.)

All documents in a foreign language must be accompanied by a notarized translation

24

Document

Check Here

FROM THE PETITIONER (U.S. CITIZEN):

1)Form I-129F

Petition for Alien Fiancé

Completed & Signed

_____

2)A written statement describing the circumstances under which you and your

Fiancé met and your intention to marry within 90 days of her arrival._____

3)Copy of U.S Birth Certificate or Naturalization Certificate

_____

4)Copy of U.S. Passport

_____

5)Proof of termination of any prior marriages (copy)

_____

25

6)Two USCIS Color Photographs (see specification sheet)

_____

7)Evidence that you have met and evidence of the relationship:

•Letters

_____

•Emails

_____

•Telephone Bills

_____

•Photographs together

_____

•Receipt from engagement ring(if available)

_____

•Visa stamps in passport from visiting fiancé

_____

•Copies of airline tickets from visiting fiancé

_____

FROM THE BENEFICIARY (FIANCÉ):

1)Two USCIS Color Photographs

_____

26

2)Proof of termination of any prior marriages, if any (copy)

_____

Your Fiancé will need the following documents for her interview at the Embassy:

- ✓ Completed Copy of Form DS-160, Online Nonimmigrant Visa Application and Confirmation Page.
- ✓ Any and all originals of documents submitted in connection with the visa petition, such as U.S petitioner's birth certificate and proof of any previous marriages were legally ended
- ✓ Fiancé passport valid for at least six months beyond the intended period of stay in the U.S.
- ✓ Police Certificates from your present country of residence and all countires where you have lived for six months or more sicne age 16
- ✓ Results of Medical Examination, in an unopended envelope
- ✓ Completed Form I-134, Affidavit of Support with supporting documentation such as proof of U.S. citizen's employment, copy of U.S. citizen's most recent federal tax returns, copy of paycheck stub and letter from U.S. citizen's bank(s) confirming the account
- ✓ Fiancé original birth certificate
- ✓ Passport-Style Photos (2)
- ✓ Evidence of any previous marriages have been terminated

- ✓ Evidence of bona fide relationship with the U.S. citizen petitioner
- ✓ Visa Fees, which is also called the "machine readable visa" (MRV) fee – (currently $265) online
- ✓ Any other documents specifically requested

Original documents bearing the signatures and seals of the issuing authorities are required at the interview.

Any documents in a foreign language must be accompanied by a Notarized English translation.

Step 2: Completing the Forms

After you have begun to gather the required supporting documents, you may now begin to complete the required USCIS forms.

The Form # is written on the bottom left-hand corner of the Form. The Form Name is written on the upper right-hand corner of the Form.

The U.S. Citizen must complete and sign the following forms:

•Form I-129F – Petition for Alien Fiancé.

•I-134 – Affidavit of Support.

I-134 Affidavit of Support – U.S. Citizen

To be completed and signed by the U.S. Citizen

Notes:

28

1)The purpose of this Form is to assure the U.S. Government that you (the U.S. Citizen) will be able to support your fiancé until she is authorized to work legally in the U.S.

2)The most widely used method of determining the ability to support is the 125% of the Poverty Line Rule. See the Poverty Guidelines in Appendix II. The Sponsors Household Size includes the number of persons related to you (the U.S. Citizen) by birth, marriage or adoption, yourself, your fiancé and her /him children that will be joining her / him.

3)The original version is to be sent to your fiancé for her / him to take to the interview.

Step 3: Sending the Application to the USCIS

Writing the Relationship Letter

The purpose of this letter is to convince the USCIS that you have met your fiancé and that your relationship is legitimate and valid. You should send your fiancé a copy of this letter as the Consular Officer may refer to it in the interview. Below is a sample letter:

Dear Immigration Officer,

I first met Diana through an Internet chat room in April 2009. We quickly found that we shared many common interests and values. After about three months of emailing each other, I decided I had to hear what her voice sounded like. We spoke on the telephone and emailed each other for another two months until I realized I was falling in love. I visited her in Warsaw in September of 2009. We spent two fabulous weeks together. Before I left to come back to the States, I asked Diana to marry me. She said yes before I could finish my sentence. I can't wait to get Diana here and marry her. Please expedite this petition

Sincerely,

David J. Johnson

Preparing the Cover Letter

Now that you have the USCIS forms completed and the required supporting documents in hand, it's time to prepare the application package and send it to the USCIS Regional Service Center.

First, you will want to write a cover letter. Use the sample below as a guide.

Sample Cover Letter

Monday, August 04, 2014

USCIS Attn: I-129F

2501 South State Highway 121 Business

Suite 400

Lewisville, TX 75067

Re:

Case Type: I-129F – K-1 Fiance Visa Petitioner: David J. JOHNSON Beneficiary: Diana NOVATNA - Fiancé

Beneficiary: Natalia GARDIMOV – Daughter of Fiancé, will apply for K-2 Visa Consulate to be notified of the approved petition: Warsaw, Poland

Note: Please cable the approval to the American Consulate in Warsaw. Dear Sir / Madam,

Please find enclosed all necessary forms and supporting documents for this I-129F petition including a check for $535 (current fee) and the following:

David J. JOHNSON – U.S. Citizen:

•Form I-129F - completed and signed

•2 USCIS Color Photos

•Copy of Birth Certificate

•Copy of Picture Page in Passport

•Copy of Divorce Decree

31

•Copy of visa stamps in passport from nvisit to Warsaw

•Letter detailing how we met and intention to marry

•Copy of Receipt for engagement ring

•Pictures Together

•Copy of Airline Ticket from visiting Warsaw

•Copies of letters and email correspondence

Diana NOVATNA – Alien Fiancé

•2 USCIS Color Photos

•Copy of Divorce Decree

Please process this petition as quickly as possible. Thank you in advance for your assistance. Respectfully yours,

David J. Johnson

Mailing the Application Package to the USCIS

Second, make copies of all the forms and documents you will be sending the USCIS.

The USCIS Dallas Lockbox For U.S. Postal Service:

USCIS

P.O. Box 660151 Dallas, TX 75266

For Express mail and courier deliveries:

USCIS Attn: I-129F

2501 South State Highway 121 Business

Suite 400

Lewisville, TX 75067

Step 4: Obtaining the Approval from the USCIS

Obtaining the I-797C Notice of Action

About 2-4 weeks after you mail in your application package, the USCIS Regional Service Center will mail you a Form I-797C Notice of Action.

This receipt will have 3 important items:

1)Your Receipt Number: This 13-digit number starts with 3 letters. It is found in the upper left-hand corner of the Form. This number must be used with all correspondence with the USCIS concerning your case.

2)The Approximate Processing Time

3)The Customer Service Telephone Number: This telephone number connects you with an automated system to check the status of your case 24 hours a day. This number is most likely going to be busy if you call during business hours. Call in the evening or early morning. You will hear a voice message detailing the status of your case. It will say one of three things:

a)We have received your petition and are processing it. We will have a decision within xx to xx days.

b)We have sent you a request for additional evidence.

c)We have sent you an approval notice and forward the case the American Consulate listed in the petition.

A sample I-797 Notice of Action - Notice of Receipt is in Appendix 3

Receiving a Request for Evidence

If you follow the guidelines in this kit, you will receive an Approval Notice from the USCIS. However if you mistakenly leave something out, the USCIS will not reject your petition, they will simply send you a Request for Evidence.

The request for evidence will be very specific. You will typically have 90 days to submit the evidence requested.

Simply send in the document(s) or Form(s) requested along with the original Request for Evidence and the USCIS will complete the processing of your petition.

Obtaining the I-797 Notice of Approval

Depending on the processing time of the USCIS Regional Service Center, you should receive the USCIS Notice of Approval within 20-90 days after they receive it. As of this printing, the Vermont Service Center is the quickest, followed by California, Texas, and Nebraska.

The USCIS Service Center will forward your approved petition to the American Consulate listed on your petition.

They USCIS Service Center will send your approved petition to the American Consulate. A sample I-797 Notice of Action .

Step 5: NVC to Consular Processing

If your fiancé security check comes back clean, your approved K1 visa petition will be routed to the Bureau of Consular Affairs. The Bureau of Consular Affairs will send your file to the U.S Embassy in your fiancé country. Usually at this stage, the fiancé will start filling out and submit Form DS-160 online at the Consular Electronic Application Center website, https://ceac.state.gov/genniv. Please note that even though your spouse did not have to file a separate I-129F petition for any children, you will usually need to file a separate DS-160 for each of them to get a K2 visa.

After receiving your visa petition, the U.S Embassy (usually in the country of origin) sends the fiancé a letter with instructions for scheduling the medical exam and interview. The petitioner (U.S. citizen) usually does not attend the embassy interview.

Each U.S Embassy or consular post has different procedures, so listen only to what your consulate tells you to do.

Usually in this letter provided by the U.S. Embassy the fiancé will need to bring to the interview at least following items:

- ✓ Completed Copy of Form DS-160, Online Nonimmigrant Visa Application and Confirmation Page.
- ✓ Any and all originals of documents submitted in connection with the visa petition, such as U.S petitioner's birth certificate and proof of any previous marriages were legally ended
- ✓ Fiancé passport valid for at least six months beyond the intended period of stay in the U.S.
- ✓ Police Certificates from your present country of residence and all countires where you have lived for six months or more sicne age 16
- ✓ Results of Medical Examination, in an unopended envelope

- ✓ Completed Form I-134, Affidavit of Support with supporting documentation such as proof of U.S. citizen's employment, copy of U.S. citizen's most recent federal tax returns, and letter from U.S. citizen's bank(s) confirming the account
- ✓ Fiancé original birth certificate
- ✓ Passport-Style Photos (2)
- ✓ Evidence of any previous marriages have been terminated
- ✓ Evidence of bona fide relationship with the U.S. citizen petitioner
- ✓ Visa Fees, which is also called the "machine readable visa" (MRV) fee – (currently $265) online
- ✓ Any other documents specifically requested

Make sure you make mulitiple copies of each of the above. One for yourself, one for the interview and one to keep at home.

Vaccination Requirements

Recent changes to United States immigration law now require immigrant visa applicants to obtain certain vaccinations (listed below) prior to the issuance of an immigrant visa.

Panel physicians who conduct medical examinations of immigrant visa applicants are now required to verify that immigrant visa applicants have met the new vaccination requirement, or that it is medically inappropriate for the visa applicant to receive one or more of the listed vaccinations:

•Mumps

•Measles

•Rubella

•polio

•tetanus and diphtheria toxoids

•pertussis

•influenzae type b (Hib)

•hepatitis B

•varicella

•pneumococcal and

•influenza

In order to assist the panel physician, and to avoid delays in the processing of an immigrant visa, all immigrant visa applicants should have their vaccination records available for the panel physician's review at the time of the immigrant medical examination.

Visa applicants should consult with their regular health care provider to obtain a copy of their immunization record, if one is available. If you do not have a vaccination record, the panel physician will work with you to determine which vaccinations you may need to meet the requirement.

Certain waivers of the vaccination requirement are available upon the recommendation of the panel physician. Only a physician can determine which of the listed vaccinations are medically appropriate for you, given your age, medical history and current medical condition.

Step 6: Scheduling an interview

The Embassy will send out a Packet explaining the process of obtaining medical exams and scheduling an appointment for a visa interview. Again, the U.S Embassy (usually in the country of origin) sends the fiancé a letter with instructions for scheduling the medical exam and interview. The petitioner (U.S. citizen) usually does not attend the embassy interview. The U.S. Embassy will instruct the Fiancé to return some of the documents immediately. Other documents will be kept until the interview.

Step 7: The Visa Interview

On the date of the appointment your fiancé should go to the Immigrant Visa Section of the Embassy.

Minor children under 14 part of the petition usually do not need to attend the interview. But it is always important to bring them.

Your fiancé, if have not already, may need to fill out a Nonimmigrant Visa Application (DS-160) in duplicate.

Each dependent child will also need Nonimmigrant Visa Applications in duplicate. Original documents, not copies, should be brought to the interview.

Originals of primary documents, such as birth, marriage, and death records, will be returned to the applicant after the interview.

The fiancé will likely be asked to present:

- ✓ Completed Copy of Form DS-160, Online Nonimmigrant Visa Application and Confirmation Page.
- ✓ Any and all originals of documents submitted in connection with the visa petition, such as U.S petitioner's birth certificate and proof of any previous marriages were legally ended
- ✓ Fiancé passport valid for at least six months beyond the intended period of stay in the U.S.
- ✓ Police Certificates from your present country of residence and all countires where you have lived for six months or more sicne age 16
- ✓ Medical exam results for the beneficiary and any dependent children
- ✓ Completed Form I-134, Affidavit of Support with supporting documentation such as proof of U.S. citizen's employment, copy of U.S. citizen's most recent federal tax returns, and letter from U.S. citizen's bank(s) confirming the account
- ✓ Fiancé original birth certificate
- ✓ Passport-Style Photos (2)
- ✓ Evidence of any previous marriages have been terminated
- ✓ Evidence of bona fide relationship with the U.S. citizen petitioner. This documentation is the

pictures together, emails, letters, engagement ring receipt, relationship letter, etc.
- ✓ Visa Fees, which is also called the "machine readable visa" (MRV) fee – (currently $265) online
- ✓ Valid passports for the beneficiary and any dependent children Birth certificates for the beneficiary and any dependent children
- ✓ Any other documents specifically requested

After a consular officer has reviewed the case, the fiancé will be interviewed.The consular officer will likely ask your fiancé questions about your relationship, such as how you met and when you decided to marry. The consular officer is required by law to verify that your relationship with your fiancé is real and that you do intend to marry within 90 days of your fiancé's arrival in the United States.

Provided everything is in order at the time of the interview, your fiancé may receive a visa the same day. And if you have not already, the fiancé and each dependent child will pay a non- refundable machine-readable-visa (MRV)- currently ($265) fee on the day of the interview. For citizens of countries that charge an extra fee to U.S. citizens seeking to go there, there may also be an additional fee the fiancé may pay called a "reciporcity fee."

Thereafter, supporting documentation, including the K petition, birth certificate, Nonimmigrant Visa Application, and medical exam will be placed in a sealed envelope and given to the applicant for presentation to USCIS at the port of entry for the fiancé to present at the Point of Entry into the United States.

Step 8: Arriving in the U.S.

When your fiancé arrives in the U.S., it is important to get legally married as soon as possible and get the application for pernanent residency started. Upon receiving the marriage certificate is usually a good rule of thumb to start the adjustment of status application process.

Step 9: How to Adjust Status to Permanent Resident and Obtain a Conditional Green Card

The process below is simply meant to be an overview of the process of applying for adjustment of status. For a more detailed version see the upcoming book: "How to apply for and obtain a Green Card by Marriage to a U.S. Citizen."

Step1: Marry within 90 days and obtain a marriage certificate.

Step 2: File for Adjustment of Status with your local USCIS office.

File the following USCIS Forms: I-129F Approval

I-485 - Application to Register Permanent Residence or Adjust Status

42

I-765 – Work Authorization

I-864 – Affidavit of Support

I-693 - Medical Examination Form

I-131 – Advance Parole - optional

Step 3: You will obtain work authorization within 90 days. You will also obtain an interview date, which will be approximately 12 months from the date of filing.

Step 4: At the interview the alien spouse will receive a conditional Green Card.

Step 5: Within 90 days of 2 years after the interview, you may file form I-751 with the USCIS, which is an application to remove conditional status.

WHO IS ELIGIBLE FOR A K-1 VISA AND HOW TO APPLY

Fiancés are fortunate in that there are no annual limits on K-1 visas, and thus no long waiting periods. The first step, fiancé visa petition approval, normally takes five to seven months. After the petition has been approved, the time it takes for the U.S. consulate to issue a visa depends partly on you, since you have to schedule your interview. If all goes as normal, you should have your visa sometime within the six-nine-month validity period of your petition.

Note: Although the accurate way to generally refer to both male and female fiancés is "fiancé(e)," we are using the term "fiancé" for simplicity's sake.

U.S. CITIZEN PETITIONERS MUST DISCLOSE CRIMINAL RECORDS

In 2005, Congress became concerned that immigrating fiancés were particularly susceptible to domestic violence and abuse—particularly those whose engagements were arranged through marriage brokers (sometimes called "mail- order brides"). In response, Congress passed the International Marriage Brokers Regulation Act (IMBRA).

As a result of IMBRA, the fiancé visa petition (Form I-129F) now asks whether you and your fiancé or spouse met through an international marriage broker. If you did, the immigrant will be asked, at the visa interview, whether the broker complied with legal requirements that he or she collect information on the U.S. fiancé or spouse's criminal record and pass it to the immigrant. USCIS must also run a criminal background check on the petitioner, and forward the information, along with the approved petition, to the U.S. Department of State, which will then send these materials to the intending immigrant.

In addition, Form I-129F now asks all U.S. citizen petitioners whether they have a history of violent crime and crime relating to alcohol or controlled- substance abuse.

SEE AN EXPERT

Do you need a lawyer? Many people are able to handle the application process for a fiancé visa on their own, without a lawyer. However, if you have any trouble dealing with paperwork or understanding the instructions, or have any complications in your case (such as a criminal record, past visa overstays in the U.S., or an immigrating child who will turn 18 soon and therefore no longer qualify as your spouse's stepchild), a lawyer is well worth the price.

DO YOU QUALIFY FOR A K-1 VISA?

The main eligibility criteria for getting a K-1 visa are:

- ✓ Your intended spouse is a U.S. citizen (not a permanent resident or green card holder).
- ✓ Both members of the couple are legally able to marry (single and of legal age).
- ✓ The immigrant must have a genuine intention to marry the U.S. citizen petitioner after arriving in the U.S. within 90 days.
- ✓ The two of you must have met and seen each other in person within the past two years before applying the petition.

This visa is not for use by couples who are simply considering marriage. In most cases, USCIS will accept a signed statement from each spouse simply stating they intend to marry the other within 90 days of the foreign spouse's arrival in the U.S. on the K-1 visa. If USCIS gets suspicious for some reason, you'll need to show proof that you truly plan to get married, such as letters to each other discussing your plans and wedding announcements to friends. One of the most convincing ways to prove this is by showing that you've actually set a date for the wedding, and made some arrangements like hiring a caterer. (But leave room for flexibility—you can't necessarily count on getting a visa in time for your planned date.)

Bringing Your Children

When you get a K-1 visa, any of your unmarried children under the age of 21 can be issued K-2 visas. This will enable them to accompany you to the U.S. They, too, will be able to apply for green cards once you get married.

For some couples, the requirement that they have already met is difficult or violates their religious principles. If you practice a religion in which marriages are customarily arranged by families and premarital meetings are prohibited, you can ask that a meeting requirement be waived. You'll have to show that both parties will be following all the customs of marriage and weddings that are part of the religion.

It is also possible to get a waiver of the personal meeting requirement if such a meeting would cause an extreme hardship to the U.S. citizen member of the couple. Only the most extreme situations involving medical problems are likely to be regarded as a good enough reason for the waiver to be granted. Economic problems alone are not usually acceptable.

You'll need to apply for a green card after the marriage separately. Although you must marry within the 90-day validity period of the K-1 visa, you may file for a green card—without leaving the United States—after the 90 days, as long as it is after you marry the U.S. citizen who petitioned for you. Just getting married does not, by itself, give you any legal status in the United States.

To maintain your legal status beyond the 90-day period, you must submit an application for adjustment of status. Because you have already gotten a K-1 visa, you are excused from the normal first step in this process (the I-130 visa petition). You will, however, be subject to the two-year conditional residency placed on green cards obtained through marriage to a U.S. citizen.

QUICK VIEW OF HOW TO APPLY FOR A K-1 VISA

Getting a K-1 visa is a four-step process:

1.Your U.S. citizen fiancé mails a visa petition on USCIS Form I-129F to the USCIS Dallas lockbox.

2. After the petition is approved, you fill out and submit a visa application form online.

3. You collect documents, and bring them to an interview at a U.S. consulate.

4.You use your K-1 fiancé visa to enter the United States.

STEP ONE: YOUR U.S. CITIZEN FIANCÉ SUBMITS A VISA PETITION

To start the process, your U.S. citizen fiancé will need to file what's called a fiancé visa petition on USCIS Form I-129F. The object of the petition is to prove that:

- ✓ You have a bona fide intention of marrying a U.S. citizen within 90 days after you arrive in the United States.
- ✓ Both of you are legally able to marry.
- ✓ You have physically met each other within the past two years—or can prove that this requirement should be waived based on religion or extreme hardship to the U.S. citizen.

The Form I-129F itself is mostly self-explanatory, but here are some tips regarding certain tricky portions based on the 03/21/22 Edition of Form I-129F.

Part 1 is for information about the U.S. citizen, and Part 2 is for information about the immigrant. Each of you will be asked your marital status. Check only one Box, and make sure it is not the one that says "married." In Part 1, Question 43, the U.S. citizen must state whether he or she has filed I-129F petitions for other immigrant fiancés or husband/wives before. If the answer is yes, USCIS will take a closer look at their and your cases to make sure this isn't a pattern that indicates fraud.

In Part 2 (your information), Question 2 asks for an "A Number (if any)." You won't have one unless you've previously applied for permanent, or in some cases temporary, residency or been in deportation/removal proceedings. (See a lawyer if that's the case.) If you have a number, you must enter it here; leave the space blank if you don't. Question 3 asks for a Social Security number. You won't have one unless you've lived in the U.S.; leave the space blank if you don't.

All of the questions about past spouses are designed to make sure both of you are free to marry now.

The address where you (the immigrating fiancé) intend to live in the U.S. should be the same as your U.S. citizen petitioner's, or you'll raise questions. If there's a compelling reason to live apart (for example, you plan to move in together only after you marry), attach a separate document explaining that.

Question 51 of Part 2 asks whether you're related to your fiancé. If the two of you are blood relations, you'll have to make sure that a marriage between you is allowed in the U.S. state where you plan to marry.

Question 55 of Part 2 requires the U.S. citizen to state whether you met through an international marriage broker, and if so, to give information about the broker.

In Question 62 of Part 2, try to name the nearest U.S. consulate with a visa processing office in your country. (Don't worry—if you get it wrong, USCIS will figure it out.)

Part 3 collects information on the U.S. citizen petitioner, who must reveal to USCIS any history of violent crime, crime relating to alcohol, or controlled substance abuse.

The petitioner should see an attorney if there is any question about whether this section applies.

The checklist below will help your U.S. citizen petitioner prepare and assemble the various forms and documents. (Note that your U.S. citizen fiancé will now be known as your "petitioner," and you are the "beneficiary.")

1.Mailing the Fiancé Visa Petition

Once your U.S. citizen petitioner has finished the fiancé visa petition, he or she must mail it to a USCIS lockbox in Dallas. Check the USCIS website at www.uscis.gov/i-129f to get the appropriate address.

2.Awaiting Approval of the Visa Petition

Within a few weeks after mailing your petition, your fiancé should get back written confirmation that the papers are being processed, together with a receipt for the fees. This notice (on Form I-797C) will also contain your immigration file number, which is useful if the decision gets delayed.

If USCIS wants further information before acting on your case, it may send your U.S. citizen petitioner a Request for Evidence (R.F.E.). This letter will tell the citizen what additional pieces of information or documents USCIS expects. He or she should mail the extra data or documents to USCIS by the deadline given.

Sometimes, USCIS will request a personal interview with the U.S. citizen petitioner prior to approving a fiancé petition. The purpose is to make sure a marriage will really take place after you arrive in the U.S. and to confirm that you have previously met each other. All interviews are held at USCIS local offices, to which your file will be forwarded before the interview. The USCIS local office will send the petitioner a notice of when and where to appear for the interview and instructions to bring additional documentation, if any is required.

Once your petition is approved, USCIS will send a Form I-797 Notice of Action to your U.S. citizen fiancé, indicating the approval. (See the sample notice below.) At the same time, USCIS will send a copy of your file to an office called the National Visa Center, which will assign you a case number and transfer the file to the appropriate U.S. consulate in your country.

CHECKLIST FOR FIANCÉ VISA PETITION

Forms and Fees

☐ Form I-129F, signed by the U.S. citizen petitioner, with accompanying fee (currently $535; check or money order, not cash). If you have children, make sure they are listed on this Form, which is necessary if you want them to accompany you.

☐ Form G-1450, if you are paying the fee by credit card. (We're describing the version of the Form dated 4/10/2017.)

Documents and Photos

☐ Proof of your fiancé's U.S. citizenship, such as a copy of his or her birth certificate, U.S. passport, certificate of citizenship, naturalization certificate, or consular record of birth abroad.

☐ Proof that you and your fiancé can legally marry, such as your birth certificate to show that you are over 18 (or whatever the age of consent is in the U.S. state where you plan to marry); and if either of you has been married before, proof that all prior marriages were legally terminated, such as a divorce decree or death certificate.

☐ Proof of your intent to marry. A simple statement from each fiancé, to this effect usually is good enough. You can include, if you wish, a statement from the U.S. citizen petitioner, describing how you met, how your relationship developed, why the two of you want to marry, and when you plan to marry. You may also include items such as wedding announcements, catering contracts, a letter or affidavit from your pastor or justice of the peace stating that he or she has been contacted about performing your marriage ceremony.

☐ Proof that you have met in person, such as photographs of the two of you together, letters you have written to each other indicating that there has been a meeting, and copies of plane tickets, credit card receipts, and hotel receipts.

☐ If you have not met each other for religious reasons, evidence of your membership in such a religion, including a letter from an official in your religious organization verifying that you and your fiancé are members, and a detailed statement from a clergyperson explaining the religious laws concerning marriage. A letter from your parents would also be helpful.

☐ If you have not met each other because it would impose an extreme hardship on your U.S. citizen petitioner, a written statement explaining in detail why you cannot meet. If there is a medical reason why the U.S. citizen can't travel to meet you, include a letter from a medical doctor explaining the condition.

☐ If the U.S. citizen petitioner has been convicted of any of the crimes listed in the instructions to Form I-129F, certified copies of the court and police records (but get a lawyer for help with your case).

☐   One photograph of you and one photograph of your U.S. citizen fiancé, in U.S. passport style, in color. Don't submit old photos; give them ones that are less than 30 days old. Write your name in pencil or felt pen on the back of your photo.

☐   If you or your fiancé is now known by a name different than the one appearing on any document you submitted, a copy of the legal document that made the change, such as a marriage certificate, adoption decree, or court order.

CAUTION

Don't use the approved fiancé visa petition to try to enter the United States! An approved petition does not by itself give you any immigration benefits. It is only a prerequisite to the next step, submitting your application at a U.S. consulate.

STEP TWO: YOU APPLY AT A U.S. CONSULATE

The consular post will send you a letter listing the documents it needs to see in order to issue you a K-1 visa, along with instructions on where to get the required medical exam and how to schedule an interview with a consular officer.

Each consular post has different procedures, so listen only to what your Consulate tells you to do.

1.Submit Nonimmigrant Visa Application Form Online:

54

All applicants for a K-1 visa must fill out and submit Form DS-160 online at the Consular Electronic Application Center website, https://ceac.state.gov/genniv. It's a lengthy form, but don't worry—if you can't finish it all in one sitting, you can save what you've done and come back to it. Make sure you note your Application ID number—you'll need it to get back to your Form.

Even though your spouse did not have to file a separate I-129F petition for any children, you will need to file a separate DS-160 for each of them to get a K-2 visa.

2.Pay Your Fees and Schedule Your Interview:

Procedures vary depending on the consular post, but often there is a way to schedule your interview and pay the application fee—also called a "machine readable visa" (M.R.V.) fee—(currently $265) online. In any case, follow the instructions for how the Consulate requires you to schedule an interview (the Consulate might do this itself) and to pay. For citizens of countries that charge an extra fee to U.S. citizens seeking to go there, there may be an additional fee called a "reciprocity fee," which typically is paid the day of the interview.

A separate fee is charged for each visa application (K-1 or K-2).

CAUTION

Your approved fiancé petition has a time limit. It can be used to get a K-1 visa only within four months of the date the petition was approved. If the process is going slowly and it looks like you won't be able to get your visa within four months, it is very important that you contact the Consulate and ask that it extend the validity period of your petition. Most consulates will agree to do this without a problem, unless they think you're to blame for the delay.

3.Preparing for Your Interview:

See the checklist below to help you organize the documents necessary for your fiancé visa interview. This checklist shows documents that are commonly required. Your Consulate may require others.

Here's some additional information regarding some of the items on the checklist below.

Police clearance. Unlike applications made in the U.S., you personally must collect police clearance certificates from each country you have lived in for one year or more since your 16th birthday. Additionally, you must have a police certificate from your home country or country of last residence, if you lived there for at least six months since the age of 16. Also, if you have ever been arrested, no matter when, you'll need a certificate from the country in which the arrest took place. You do not need to obtain police certificates from the United States, or from countries where police certificates are never issued or are considered unreliable.

56

CHECKLIST FOR FIANCÉ VISA INTERVIEW

Forms

☐ USCIS Form I-134, Affidavit of Support, if the Consulate requests it (signed by the U.S. petitioner, stating that he or she will reimburse the government if you receive public assistance or welfare).

Documents

☐ Printed confirmation page from your online DS-160 application.

☐ Originals of documents submitted in connection with the visa petition, such as your fiancé's U.S. birth certificate and proof that any previous marriages were legally ended.

☐ Documents to accompany Form I-134, such as proof of U.S. citizen's employment, copy of U.S. citizen's most recent federal tax return, and letter from U.S. citizen's bank(s) confirming the account(s).

☐ A valid passport from your home country, good for at least six months.

☐ Your original birth certificate.

☐ An original police clearance certificate, if available in your country (the instructions from the Consulate will tell you).

☐ Two additional photographs of you, the immigrating fiancé (according to the Consulate's photo instructions).

- ☐ Results of your medical examination, in an unopened envelope.
- ☐ Additional documents proving your relationship (to cover the time since you submitted the fiancé visa petition), such as phone bills showing calls to one another, copies of emails and other correspondence, and photos taken during recent joint vacations.
- ☐ Fee receipt showing that you have paid the relevant visa application fee (currently $265). The method of payment depends on the country. Check the website of the U.S. consulate where you plan to apply for your visa to learn how and where your fee can be paid in advance. Most consulates will not allow you to pay the visa fee at the time of interview.
- ☐ Fingerprints, if requested by the consulate.

The State Department's website, www.travel.state.gov, contains instructions on how to obtain police certificates from every country. (Search for "Reciprocity and Civil Documents by Country.") The website will tell you which countries don't have police certificates at all.

Some countries will send certificates directly to U.S. consulates but not to you personally. Before they send the certificates out, however, you must request that it be done. Usually this requires filing some type of request form, together with a set of your fingerprints.

Fingerprints. A few consulates require you to submit fingerprints, though most do not. Consulates wanting fingerprints will send you instructions.

Photos. You must bring to the interview two photographs of you and two photographs of each accompanying child. They must be taken in compliance with the Consulate's instructions (U.S "passport style"). Many photographers are familiar with U.S. passport style. If you're a do-it- yourself type, passport-style specifications are available on the State Department's website, www.travel.state.gov. If your religious beliefs require wearing a head covering, you should be able to keep it on for the photo. However, your full face must be visible and your head covering cannot obscure your hairline or cast shadows on your face. You can't be wearing eyeglasses.

Medical exam. Immediately before your visa interview, you and any accompanying children will be required to have medical examinations. Some consulates conduct the medical exams up to several days before the interview. Others schedule the medical exam and the interview on the same day. You will be told where to go and what to do in your appointment letter.

The medical examinations are conducted by private doctors. The fees depend on the doctor and country. The exam itself involves taking a medical history, blood test, and chest X-ray and administering vaccinations, if required. Pregnant women can refuse to be X-rayed until after the pregnancy. The vaccination requirement may be waived for religious, moral, or medical reasons. You also have the option to postpone your vaccinations until you're ready to apply for adjustment of status.

The main purpose of the medical exam is to verify that you are not medically inadmissible. Some medical grounds of inadmissibility can be overcome with treatment or by applying for a waiver. If you need a medical waiver, you will be given complete instructions by the Consulate at the time of your interview, but should also consult an experienced immigration attorney.

Affidavit of support. As part of overcoming the grounds of inadmissibility, you will have to show that you will not become a public charge (need government assistance) in the U.S. while you're in K-1 status. Normally, the Consulate will ask the U.S. fiancé to fill out an Affidavit of Support on Form I-134. The I-134 is simpler than the I-864 Affidavit of Support form (discussed in Chapter 3), and is not considered legally enforceable. In other words, the U.S. government is very unlikely to go after your U.S. citizen fiancé for reimbursement if you end up needing public benefits. If your U.S. citizen fiancé does not make enough money to support you, you should submit an additional I-134 from a U.S.-based family member of your U.S. citizen fiancé and hope that satisfies the Consulate that you won't become a public charge.

4.Attending Your Interview:

After the medical exam, you and your accompanying children will report to the Consulate for the interview. Bring with you to the interview the items on the checklist above and anything else the Consulate requested. The interview process involves verification of your application's accuracy and an inspection of your documents.

Step Three: You Enter the U.S. on Your Fiancé Visa

Normally, you must use the visa to enter the U.S. within six months, though the Consulate can extend this period if necessary. The inspection process involves a U.S. border officer opening the sealed envelope containing your visa documents, and doing a last check to make sure you haven't used fraud. The border officer has expedited removal powers, which means he or she can turn you right around and send you home if anything appears wrong in your packet or with your answers to the officer's questions. Be polite and careful in answering.

When the officer is satisfied that everything is in order, he or she will stamp your passport to show that you're now a K-1 visa holder, and you will be authorized to remain in the U.S. for 90 days. If you are bringing accompanying children, they must enter the U.S. at either the same time or after you do.

If you're planning to apply for a green card, your most important task at this point is to get married. You can't apply for the green card until you have an official government certificate of your marriage, which sometimes takes weeks after the wedding to be prepared. For more information on applying to adjust status based on your marriage.

SAMPLE PETITION FOR ALIEN FIANCÉ(E)

SAMPLE PETITION FOR ALIEN FIANCÉ(E): FORMS G-28 AND I-129F

**Notice of Entry of Appearance
as Attorney or Accredited Representative**

Department of Homeland Security

**DHS
Form G-28**
OMB No. 1615-0105
Expires 05/31/2021

Part 1. Information About Attorney or Accredited Representative

1. USCIS Online Account Number (if any)

   ▶ [blank]

Name of Attorney or Accredited Representative

2.a. Family Name (Last Name)   Howe

2.b. Given Name (First Name)   Barry

2.c. Middle Name   [blank]

Address of Attorney or Accredited Representative

3.a. Street Number and Name   1234 Court Street

3.b. ☐ Apt. ☐ Ste. ☐ Flr.   [blank]

3.c. City or Town   Marietta

3.d. State GA   3.e. ZIP Code 30008

3.f. Province   N/A

3.g. Postal Code   N/A

3.h. Country

United States

Contact Information of Attorney or Accredited Representative

4. Daytime Telephone Number

   5555555555

5. Mobile Telephone Number (if any)

   N/A

6. Email Address (if any)

   fakelawyer@fakelawfirm.com

7. Fax Number (if any)

   5555556666

Part 2. Eligibility Information for Attorney or Accredited Representative

Select **all applicable** items.

1.a. ☒ I am an attorney eligible to practice law in, and a member in good standing of, the bar of the highest courts of the following states, possessions, territories, commonwealths, or the District of Columbia. If you need extra space to complete this section, use the space provided in **Part 6. Additional Information**.

   Licensing Authority

   GA

1.b. Bar Number (if applicable)

   234567

1.c. I (select **only one** box) ☒ am not ☐ am subject to any order suspending, enjoining, restraining, disbarring, or otherwise restricting me in the practice of law. If you are subject to any orders, use the space provided in **Part 6. Additional Information** to provide an explanation.

1.d. Name of Law Firm or Organization (if applicable)

   Dewey Cheetum and Howe Law Firm

2.a. ☐ I am an accredited representative of the following qualified nonprofit religious, charitable, social service, or similar organization established in the United States and recognized by the Department of Justice in accordance with 8 CFR part 1292.

2.b. Name of Recognized Organization

   [blank]

2.c. Date of Accreditation (mm/dd/yyyy)

   [blank]

3. ☐ I am associated with

   [blank]

   the attorney or accredited representative of record who previously filed Form G-28 in this case, and my appearance as an attorney or accredited representative for a limited purpose is at his or her request.

4.a. ☐ I am a law student or law graduate working under the direct supervision of the attorney or accredited representative of record on this form in accordance with the requirements in 8 CFR 292.1(a)(2).

4.b. Name of Law Student or Law Graduate

   [blank]

63

Part 3. Notice of Appearance as Attorney or Accredited Representative

If you need extra space to complete this section, use the space provided in **Part 6. Additional Information**.

This appearance relates to immigration matters before (select **only one** box):

1.a. ☒ U.S. Citizenship and Immigration Services (USCIS)

1.b. List the form numbers or specific matter in which appearance is entered.

I-129F

2.a. ☐ U.S. Immigration and Customs Enforcement (ICE)

2.b. List the specific matter in which appearance is entered.

3.a. ☐ U.S. Customs and Border Protection (CBP)

3.b. List the specific matter in which appearance is entered.

4. Receipt Number (if any)

▶

5. I enter my appearance as an attorney or accredited representative at the request of the (select **only one** box):

☐ Applicant ☒ Petitioner ☐ Requestor
☐ Beneficiary/Derivative ☐ Respondent (ICE, CBP)

Information About Client (Applicant, Petitioner, Requestor, Beneficiary or Derivative, Respondent, or Authorized Signatory for an Entity)

6.a. Family Name (Last Name) Murphy

6.b. Given Name (First Name) Samuel

6.c. Middle Name

7.a. Name of Entity (if applicable)

N/A

7.b. Title of Authorized Signatory for Entity (if applicable)

N/A

8. Client's USCIS Online Account Number (if any)

▶

9. Client's Alien Registration Number (A-Number) (if any)

▶ A-

Client's Contact Information

10. Daytime Telephone Number

5555551111

11. Mobile Telephone Number (if any)

5555551111

12. Email Address (if any)

fakeclient@fakeclient.com

Mailing Address of Client

NOTE: Provide the client's mailing address. **Do not** provide the business mailing address of the attorney or accredited representative **unless** it serves as the safe mailing address on the application or petition being filed with this Form G-28.

13.a. Street Number and Name 1234 Main Street

13.b. ☐ Apt. ☐ Ste. ☐ Flr.

13.c. City or Town Peoria

13.d. State IL **13.e.** ZIP Code 61604

13.f. Province N/A

13.g. Postal Code N/A

13.h. Country

United States

Part 4. Client's Consent to Representation and Signature

Consent to Representation and Release of Information

I have requested the representation of and consented to being represented by the attorney or accredited representative named in **Part 1.** of this form. According to the Privacy Act of 1974 and U.S. Department of Homeland Security (DHS) policy, I also consent to the disclosure to the named attorney or accredited representative of any records pertaining to me that appear in any system of records of USCIS, ICE, or CBP.

Part 4. Client's Consent to Representation and Signature (continued)

Options Regarding Receipt of USCIS Notices and Documents

USCIS will send notices to both a represented party (the client) and his, her, or its attorney or accredited representative either through mail or electronic delivery. USCIS will send all secure identity documents and Travel Documents to the client's U.S. mailing address.

If you want to have notices and/or secure identity documents sent to your attorney or accredited representative of record rather than to you, please select **all applicable** items below. You may change these elections through written notice to USCIS.

1.a. ☒ I request that USCIS send original notices on an application or petition to the business address of my attorney or accredited representative as listed in this form.

1.b. ☒ I request that USCIS send any secure identity document (Permanent Resident Card, Employment Authorization Document, or Travel Document) that I receive to the U.S. business address of my attorney or accredited representative (or to a designated military or diplomatic address in a foreign country (if permitted)).

   NOTE: If your notice contains Form I-94, Arrival-Departure Record, USCIS will send the notice to the U.S. business address of your attorney or accredited representative. If you would rather have your Form I-94 sent directly to you, select **Item Number 1.c.**

1.c. ☐ I request that USCIS send my notice containing Form I-94 to me at my U.S. mailing address.

Signature of Client or Authorized Signatory for an Entity

2.a. Signature of Client or Authorized Signatory for an Entity

➡ [_____]

2.b. Date of Signature (mm/dd/yyyy) [_____]

Part 5. Signature of Attorney or Accredited Representative

I have read and understand the regulations and conditions contained in 8 CFR 103.2 and 292 governing appearances and representation before DHS. I declare under penalty of perjury under the laws of the United States that the information I have provided on this form is true and correct.

1. a. Signature of Attorney or Accredited Representative

[_____]

1.b. Date of Signature (mm/dd/yyyy) [_____]

2.a. Signature of Law Student or Law Graduate

[_____]

2.b. Date of Signature (mm/dd/yyyy) [_____]

65

Part 6. Additional Information

If you need extra space to provide any additional information within this form, use the space below. If you need more space than what is provided, you may make copies of this page to complete and file with this form or attach a separate sheet of paper. Type or print your name at the top of each sheet; indicate the **Page Number**, **Part Number**, and **Item Number** to which your answer refers; and sign and date each sheet.

1.a Family Name
(Last Name)

1.b. Given Name
(First Name)

1.c. Middle Name

2.a. Page Number   **2.b.** Part Number   **2.c.** Item Number

2.d.

3.a. Page Number   **3.b.** Part Number   **3.c.** Item Number

3.d.

4.a. Page Number   **4.b.** Part Number   **4.c.** Item Number

4.d.

5.a. Page Number   **5.b.** Part Number   **5.c.** Item Number

5.d.

6.a. Page Number   **6.b.** Part Number   **6.c.** Item Number

6.d.

Petition for Alien Fiancé(e)

Department of Homeland Security
U.S. Citizenship and Immigration Services

**USCIS
Form I-129F**
OMB No. 1615-0001
Expires 07/31/2022

For USCIS Use Only		Fee Stamp		Action Block

Case ID Number

A-Number

G-28 Number

☐ The petition is approved for status under Section 101(a)(15)(K). It is valid for 4 months and expires on: _____	**Extraordinary Circumstances Waiver**	
	☐ Approved	Reason _____
	☐ Denied	

General Waiver		Mandatory Waiver	
☐ Approved	Reason _____	☐ Approved	Reason _____
☐ Denied		☐ Denied	

AMCON: _____

☐ Personal Interview   ☐ Previously Forwarded

☐ Document Check   ☐ Field Investigation

Initial Receipt	Relocated	Completed	Remarks
	Received	Approved	
Resubmitted	Sent	Returned	

IMBRA disclosure to the beneficiary required?
☐ Yes ☐ No

▶ **START HERE - Type or print in black ink.**

Part 1. Information About You

1. Alien Registration Number (A-Number) (if any)

   ▶ A-

2. USCIS Online Account Number (if any)

   ▶

3. U.S. Social Security Number (if any)

   ▶ 1 2 3 4 5 6 7 8 9

Select **one** box below to indicate the classification you are requesting for your beneficiary:

4.a. ☒ Fiancé(e) (K-1 visa)

4.b. ☐ Spouse (K-3 visa)

5. If you are filing to classify your spouse as a K-3, have you filed Form I-130?   ☐ Yes   ☐ No

Your Full Name

6.a. Family Name (Last Name) **Murphy**

6.b. Given Name (First Name) **Samuel**

6.c. Middle Name

Other Names Used

Provide all other names you have ever used, including aliases, maiden name, and nicknames. If you need extra space to complete this section, use the space provided in **Part 8. Additional Information.**

7.a. Family Name (Last Name) **N/A**

7.b. Given Name (First Name)

7.c. Middle Name

Your Mailing Address   *(USPS ZIP Code Lookup)*

8.a. In Care Of Name

8.b. Street Number and Name **1234 Main Street**

8.c. ☐ Apt.   ☐ Ste.   ☐ Flr.

8.d. City or Town **Peoria**

8.e. State **IL**   8.f. ZIP Code **61604**

8.g. Province **N/A**

8.h. Postal Code **N/A**

8.i. Country **United States**

8.j. Is your current mailing address the same as your physical address?   ☒ Yes   ☐ No

If you answered "No," provide your physical address in **Item Numbers 9.a. - 9.h.**

Part 1. Information About You (continued)

Your Address History

Provide your physical addresses for the last five years, whether inside or outside the United States. Provide your current address first if it is different from your mailing address in **Item Numbers 8.a. - 8.i.** If you need extra space to complete this section, use the space provided in **Part 8. Additional Information.**

Physical Address 1

9.a. Street Number and Name | 1234 Main Street

9.b. ☐ Apt. ☐ Ste. ☐ Flr.

9.c. City or Town | Peoria

9.d. State | IL **9.e.** ZIP Code | 61604

9.f. Province | N/A

9.g. Postal Code | N/A

9.h. Country | United States

10.a. Date From (mm/dd/yyyy) | 08/01/2011

10.b. Date To (mm/dd/yyyy) | PRESENT

Physical Address 2

11.a. Street Number and Name

11.b. ☐ Apt. ☐ Ste. ☐ Flr.

11.c. City or Town

11.d. State | **11.e.** ZIP Code

11.f. Province

11.g. Postal Code

11.h. Country

12.a. Date From (mm/dd/yyyy)

12.b. Date To (mm/dd/yyyy)

Your Employment History

Provide your employment history for the last five years, whether inside or outside the United States. Provide your current employment first. If you need extra space to complete this section, use the space provided in **Part 8. Additional Information.**

Employer 1

13. Full Name of Employer

Peoria Hospital

14.a. Street Number and Name | 555 Hospital Drive

14.b. ☐ Apt. ☒ Ste. ☐ Flr. | 101

14.c. City or Town | Peoria

14.d. State | IL **14.e.** ZIP Code | 61604

14.f. Province | N/A

14.g. Postal Code | N/A

14.h. Country | United States

15. Your Occupation (specify)

Physician

16.a. Employment Start Date (mm/dd/yyyy) | 08/01/2011

16.b. Employment End Date (mm/dd/yyyy) | Present

Employer 2

17. Full Name of Employer

18.a. Street Number and Name

18.b. ☐ Apt. ☐ Ste. ☐ Flr.

18.c. City or Town

18.d. State | **18.e.** ZIP Code

18.f. Province

18.g. Postal Code

18.h. Country

19. Your Occupation (specify)

Part 1. Information About You (continued)

20.a. Employment Start Date
(mm/dd/yyyy) [   ]

20.b. Employment End Date
(mm/dd/yyyy) [   ]

Other Information

21. Gender ☒ Male ☐ Female

22. Date of Birth (mm/dd/yyyy) [02/18/1986]

23. Marital Status
☒ Single ☐ Married ☐ Divorced ☐ Widowed

24. City/Town/Village of Birth
[Chicago]

25. Province or State of Birth
[IL]

26. Country of Birth
[United States]

Information About Your Parents

Parent 1's Information

27.a. Family Name
(Last Name) [Murphy]

27.b. Given Name
(First Name) [William]

27.c. Middle Name [Robert]

28. Date of Birth (mm/dd/yyyy) [01/07/1961]

29. Gender ☒ Male ☐ Female

30. Country of Birth
[United States]

31.a. City/Town/Village of Residence
[Chicago, IL]

31.b. Country of Residence
[United States]

Parent 2's Information

32.a. Family Name
(Last Name) [Murphy]

32.b. Given Name
(First Name) [Carolyn]

32.c. Middle Name [   ]

33. Date of Birth (mm/dd/yyyy) [7/2/1988]

34. Gender ☐ Male ☒ Female

35. Country of Birth
[United States]

36.a. City/Town/Village of Residence
[Chicago, IL]

36.b. Country of Residence
[United States]

37. Have you ever been previously married?
☐ Yes ☒ No

If you answered "Yes" to **Item Number 37.**, provide the names of each spouse and the date that each prior marriage ended in **Item Numbers 38.a. - 39.** If you need extra space to complete this section, use the space provided in **Part 8. Additional Information**.

Name of Previous Spouse

38.a. Family Name
(Last Name) [N/A]

38.b. Given Name
(First Name) [   ]

38.c. Middle Name [   ]

39. Date Marriage Ended (mm/dd/yyyy) [   ]

Your Citizenship Information

You are a U.S. citizen through (select only one box):

40.a. ☒ Birth in the United States

40.b. ☐ Naturalization

40.c. ☐ U.S. citizen parents

41. Have you obtained a Certificate of Naturalization or a Certificate of Citizenship in your own name?
☐ Yes ☒ No

If you answered "Yes" to **Item Number 41.**, complete **Item Numbers 42.a. - 42.c.**

Part 1. Information About You (continued)

42.a. Certificate Number

42.b. Place of Issuance

42.c. Date of Issuance (mm/dd/yyyy)

Additional Information

43. Have you ever filed Form I-129F for any other beneficiary? ☐ Yes ☒ No

If you answered "Yes" to **Item Number 43.**, provide the responses to **Item Number 44. - 46.** for each previous beneficiary. If you need to provide information for more than one beneficiary, use the space provided in **Part 8. Additional Information**.

44. A-Number (if any) ▶ A- N / A

45.a. Family Name (Last Name) N/A

45.b. Given Name (First Name)

45.c. Middle Name

46. Date of Filing (mm/dd/yyyy)

47. What action did USCIS take on Form I-129F (for example, approved, denied, revoked)?

48. Do you have any children under 18 years of age? ☐ Yes ☒ No

If you answered "Yes" to **Item Number 48.**, provide the ages for your children under 18 years of age in **Item Numbers 49.a. - 49.b.**

Provide the ages for your children under 18 years of age. If you need extra space to complete this section, use the space provided in **Part 8. Additional Information**.

49.a. Age

49.b. Age

Provide all U.S. states and foreign countries in which you have resided since your 18th birthday.

Residence 1

50.a. State IL

50.b. Country

United States

Residence 2

51.a. State

51.b. Country

Part 2. Information About Your Beneficiary

1.a. Family Name (Last Name) Rivera Rios

1.b. Given Name (First Name) Anna

1.c. Middle Name

2. A-Number (if any)

▶ A- N / A

3. U.S. Social Security Number (if any)

▶ N / A

4. Date of Birth (mm/dd/yyyy) 01/03/1990

5. Gender ☐ Male ☒ Female

6. Marital Status

☒ Single ☐ Married ☐ Divorced ☐ Widowed

7. City/Town/Village of Birth

Cortes

8. Country of Birth

Honduras

9. Country of Citizenship or Nationality

Honduras

Other Names Used

Provide all other names you have ever used, including aliases, maiden name, and nicknames. If you need extra space to complete this section, use the space provided in **Part 8. Additional Information**.

10.a. Family Name (Last Name) N/A

10.b. Given Name (First Name)

10.c. Middle Name

Part 2. Information About Your Beneficiary (continued)

Mailing Address for Your Beneficiary

11.a. In Care Of Name

11.b. Street Number and Name | APDO Postal 23

11.c. ☐ Apt. ☐ Ste. ☐ Flr.

11.d. City or Town | Cortes

11.e. State

11.f. ZIP Code

11.g. Province | San Pedro Sula

11.h. Postal Code | N/A

11.i. Country | Honduras

Your Beneficiary's Address History

Provide your beneficiary's physical addresses for the last five years, whether inside or outside the United States. Provide your beneficiary's current address first if it is different from the mailing address in **Item Numbers 11.a. - 11.i.** If you need extra space to complete this section, use the space provided in **Part 8. Additional Information.**

Beneficiary's Physical Address 1

12.a. Street Number and Name | APDO Postal 23

12.b. ☐ Apt. ☐ Ste. ☐ Flr.

12.c. City or Town | Cortes

12.d. State

12.e. ZIP Code

12.f. Province | San Pedro Sula

12.g. Postal Code | N/A

12.h. Country | Honduras

13.a. Date From (mm/dd/yyyy) | 08/01/2014

13.b. Date To (mm/dd/yyyy) | PRESENT

Beneficiary's Physical Address 2

14.a. Street Number and Name

14.b. ☐ Apt. ☐ Ste. ☐ Flr.

14.c. City or Town

14.d. State

14.e. ZIP Code

14.f. Province

14.g. Postal Code

14.h. Country

15.a. Date From (mm/dd/yyyy)

15.b. Date To (mm/dd/yyyy)

Your Beneficiary's Employment History

Provide your employment history for the last five years, whether inside or outside the United States. Provide your current employment first. If you need extra space to complete this section, use the space provided in **Part 8. Additional Information.**

Beneficiary's Employer 1

16. Full Name of Employer

Universidad De Honduras

17.a. Street Number and Name | Blvd Suyapa

17.b. ☐ Apt. ☐ Ste. ☐ Flr.

17.c. City or Town | Cortes

17.d. State

17.e. ZIP Code

17.f. Province | San Pedro Sula

17.g. Postal Code | N/A

17.h. Country | Honduras

18. Beneficiary's Occupation (specify)

Student

19.a. Employment Start Date (mm/dd/yyyy) | 08/01/2019

19.b. Employment End Date (mm/dd/yyyy) | Present

Part 2. Information About Your Beneficiary (continued)

Beneficiary's Employer 2

20. Full Name of Employer

Iglesia de Cristo

21.a. Street Number and Name

Bo. Barandillas 4A. N.e.3C

21.b. ☐ Apt. ☐ Ste. ☐ Flr.

21.c. City or Town

Cortes

21.d. State

21.e. ZIP Code

21.f. Province

San Pedro Sula

21.g. Postal Code

N/A

21.h. Country

Honduras

22. Beneficiary's Occupation (specify)

Secretary

23.a. Employment Start Date (mm/dd/yyyy)

09/01/2012

23.b. Employment End Date (mm/dd/yyyy)

05/15/2019

Information About Your Beneficiary's Parents

Parent 1's Information

24.a. Family Name (Last Name)

Rivera Hernandez

24.b. Given Name (First Name)

Carlos

24.c. Middle Name

25. Date of Birth (mm/dd/yyyy)

05/10/1963

26. Gender ☒ Male ☐ Female

27. Country of Birth

Honduras

28.a. City/Town/Village of Residence

Tegucigalpa

28.b. Country of Residence

Honduras

Parent 2's Information

29.a. Family Name (Last Name)

Rios Rodriguez

29.b. Given Name (First Name)

Vera

29.c. Middle Name

30. Date of Birth (mm/dd/yyyy)

02/19/1970

31. Gender ☐ Male ☒ Female

32. Country of Birth

Honduras

33.a. City/Town/Village of Residence

Tegucigalpa

33.b. Country of Residence

Honduras

Other Information About Your Beneficiary

34. Has your beneficiary ever been previously married?

☐ Yes ☒ No

If you answered "Yes" to **Item Number 34.,** provide the names of each prior spouse and the date each prior marriage ended in **Item Numbers 35.a. - 36.** If you need to provide information for more than one spouse, use the space provided in **Part 8. Additional Information.**

Name of Previous Spouse

35.a. Family Name (Last Name)

35.b. Given Name (First Name)

35.c. Middle Name

36. Date Marriage Ended

(mm/dd/yyyy)

37. Has your beneficiary ever been in the United States?

☒ Yes ☐ No

If your beneficiary is currently in the United States, complete **Item Numbers 38.a. - 38.h.**

38.a. He or she last entered as a (for example, visitor, student, exchange alien, crewman, stowaway, temporary worker, without inspection):

38.b. I-94 Arrival-Departure Record Number

▶

38.c. Date of Arrival (mm/dd/yyyy)

Part 2. Information About Your Beneficiary (continued)

38.d. Date authorized stay expired or will expire as shown on Form I-94 or I-95 (mm/dd/yyyy)

38.e. Passport Number

38.f. Travel Document Number

38.g. Country of Issuance for Passport or Travel Document

38.h. Expiration Date for Passport or Travel Document (mm/dd/yyyy)

39. Does your beneficiary have any children?

☐ Yes ☒ No

If you answered "Yes" to **Item Number 39.**, provide the following information about each child. If you need to provide information for more than one child, use the space provided in **Part 8. Additional Information**.

Children of Beneficiary

40.a. Family Name (Last Name) N/A

40.b. Given Name (First Name)

40.c. Middle Name

41. Country of Birth

42. Date of Birth (mm/dd/yyyy)

43. Does this child reside with your beneficiary?

☐ Yes ☐ No

If the child does not reside with your beneficiary, provide the child's physical residence.

44.a. Street Number and Name

44.b. ☐ Apt. ☐ Ste. ☐ Flr.

44.c. City or Town

44.d. State **44.e.** ZIP Code

44.f. Province

44.g. Postal Code

44.h. Country

Address in the United States Where Your Beneficiary Intends to Live

45.a. Street Number and Name 1234 Main Street

45.b. ☐ Apt. ☐ Ste. ☐ Flr.

45.c. City or Town Peoria

45.d. State IL **45.e.** ZIP Code 61604

46. Daytime Telephone Number

5555551111

Your Beneficiary's Physical Address Abroad

47.a. Street Number and Name APDO Postal 23

47.b. ☐ Apt. ☐ Ste. ☐ Flr.

47.c. City or Town Cortes

47.d. Province San Pedro Sula

47.e. Postal Code N/A

47.f. Country Honduras

48. Daytime Telephone Number

50411111111

Your Beneficiary's Name and Address in His or Her Native Alphabet

49.a. Family Name (Last Name) N/A

49.b. Given Name (First Name)

49.c. Middle Name

50.a. Street Number and Name

50.b. ☐ Apt. ☐ Ste. ☐ Flr.

50.c. City or Town

50.d. Province

50.e. Postal Code

50.f. Country

Part 2. Information About Your Beneficiary (continued)

51. Is your fiancé(e) related to you?

☐ Yes ☒ No ☐ N/A, beneficiary is my spouse

52. Provide the nature and degree of relationship (for example, third cousin or maternal uncle).

N/A

53. Have you and your fiancé(e) met in person during the two years immediately before filing this petition?

☒ Yes ☐ No ☐ N/A, beneficiary is my spouse

If you answered "Yes" to **Item Number 53.**, describe the circumstances of your in-person meeting in **Item Number 54.** Attach evidence to demonstrate that you were in each other's physical presence during the required two year period.

If you answered "No," explain your reasons for requesting an exemption from the in person meeting requirement in **Item Number 54.** and provide evidence that you should be exempt from this requirement. Refer to **Part 2., Item Numbers 53. - 54.** of the **Specific Instructions** section of the Instructions for additional information about the requirement to meet. If you need extra space to complete this section, use the space provided in **Part 8. Additional Information**.

54.

I have visited Anna in Honduras three times in the past two years: from 12/20/2019 to 1/5/2020; from 10/3/2020 to 10/17/2020; and from 1/15/2021 to 1/22/2021. See my letter for more detail of those trips.

International Marriage Broker (IMB) Information

55. Did you meet your beneficiary through the services of an IMB? ☐ Yes ☒ No

If you answered "Yes" to **Item Number 55.**, provide the IMB's contact information and Website information below. In addition, attach a copy of the signed, written consent form the IMB obtained from your beneficiary authorizing your beneficiary's personal contact information to be released to you.

56. IMB's Name (if any)

N/A

57.a. Family Name of IMB (Last Name)

57.b. Given Name of IMB (First Name)

58. Organization Name of IMB

59. Website of IMB

60.a. Street Number and Name

60.b. ☐ Apt. ☐ Ste. ☐ Flr.

60.c. City or Town

60.d. Province

60.e. Postal Code

60.f. Country

61. Daytime Telephone Number

Consular Processing Information

Your beneficiary will apply for a visa abroad at the U.S. Embassy or U.S. Consulate at:

62.a. City or Town

Tegucigalpa

62.b. Country

Honduras

Part 3. Other Information

Criminal Information

NOTE: These criminal information questions must be answered even if your records were sealed, cleared, or if anyone, including a judge, law enforcement officer, or attorney, told you that you no longer have a record. If you need extra space to complete this section, use the space provided in **Part 8. Additional Information**.

1. Have you **EVER** been subject to a temporary or permanent protection or restraining order (either civil or criminal)? ☐ Yes ☒ No

Have you EVER been arrested or convicted of any of the following crimes:

2.a. Domestic violence, sexual assault, child abuse, child neglect, dating violence, elder abuse, stalking or an attempt to commit any of these crimes? (See **Part 3. Other Information, Item Numbers 1. - 3.c.** of the Instructions for the full definition of the term "domestic violence.") ☐ Yes ☒ No

Part 3. Other Information (continued)

2.b. Homicide, murder, manslaughter, rape, abusive sexual contact, sexual exploitation, incest, torture, trafficking, peonage, holding hostage, involuntary servitude, slave trade, kidnapping, abduction, unlawful criminal restraint, false imprisonment, or an attempt to commit any of these crimes? ☐ Yes ☒ No

2.c. Three or more arrests or convictions, not from a single act, for crimes relating to a controlled substance or alcohol? ☐ Yes ☒ No

NOTE: If you were ever arrested or convicted of any of the specified crimes, you must submit certified copies of all court and police records showing the charges and disposition for every arrest or conviction. You must do so even if your records were sealed, expunged, or otherwise cleared, and regardless of whether anyone, including a judge, law enforcement officer, or attorney, informed you that you no longer have a criminal record. If you need extra space to complete this section, use the space provided in **Part 8. Additional Information**.

If you have provided information about a conviction for a crime listed in **Item Numbers 2.a. - 2.c.** and you were being battered or subjected to extreme cruelty at the time of your conviction, select all of the following that apply to you:

3.a. ☐ I was acting in self-defense.

3.b. ☐ I violated a protection order issued for my own protection.

3.c. ☐ I committed, was arrested for, was convicted of, or pled guilty to a crime that did not result in serious bodily injury and there was a connection between the crime and me having been battered or subjected to extreme cruelty.

4.a. Have you ever been arrested, cited, charged, indicted, convicted, fined, or imprisoned for breaking or violating any law or ordinance in any country, excluding traffic violations (unless a traffic violation was alcohol- or drug-related or involved a fine of $500 or more)?

☐ Yes ☒ No

4.b. If the answer to **Item Number 4.a.** is "Yes," provide information about each of those arrests, citations, charges, indictments, convictions, fines, or imprisonments in the space below. If you were the subject of an order of protection or restraining order and believe you are the victim, please explain those circumstances and provide any evidence to support your claims. Include the dates and outcomes. If you need extra space to complete this section, use the space provided in **Part 8. Additional Information**.

Multiple Filer Waiver Request Information

Refer to **Part 3. Types of Waivers** in the **Specific Instructions** section of the Instructions for an explanation of the filing waivers.

Indicate which one of the following waivers you are requesting:

5.a. ☐ Multiple Filer, No Permanent Restraining Orders or Convictions for a Specified Offense (**General Waiver**)

5.b. ☐ Multiple Filer, Prior Permanent Restraining Orders or Criminal Conviction for Specified Offense (**Extraordinary Circumstances Waiver**)

5.c. ☐ Multiple Filer, Prior Permanent Restraining Order or Criminal Convictions for Specified Offense Resulting from Domestic Violence (**Mandatory Waiver**)

5.d. ☒ Not applicable, beneficiary is my spouse or I am not a multiple filer

Part 4. Biographic Information

1. Ethnicity (Select **only one** box)

☐ Hispanic or Latino

☒ Not Hispanic or Latino

2. Race (Select **all applicable** boxes)

☒ White

☐ Asian

☐ Black or African American

☐ American Indian or Alaska Native

☐ Native Hawaiian or Other Pacific Islander

3. Height   Feet [5]   Inches [11]

4. Weight   Pounds [1] [6] [5]

5. Eye Color (Select **only one** box)

☐ Black   ☐ Blue   ☒ Brown
☐ Gray   ☐ Green   ☐ Hazel
☐ Maroon   ☐ Pink   ☐ Unknown/Other

6. Hair Color (Select **only one** box)

☐ Bald (No hair)   ☐ Black   ☐ Blond
☒ Brown   ☐ Gray   ☐ Red
☐ Sandy   ☐ White   ☐ Unknown/Other

Part 5. Petitioner's Statement, Contact Information, Declaration, Certification, and Signature

NOTE: Read the **Penalties** section of the Form I-129F Instructions before completing this part.

Petitioner's Statement

NOTE: Select the box for either **Item Number 1.a.** or **1.b.** If applicable, select the box for **Item Number 2.**

1.a. ☒ I can read and understand English, and I have read and understand every question and instruction on this petition and my answer to every question.

1.b. ☐ The interpreter named in **Part 6.** read to me every question and instruction on this petition and my answer to every question in

_____,

a language in which I am fluent, and I understood everything.

2. ☒ At my request, the preparer named in **Part 7.**,

| Barry Howe |

prepared this petition for me based only upon information I provided or authorized.

Petitioner's Contact Information

3. Petitioner's Daytime Telephone Number

| 5555551111 |

4. Petitioner's Mobile Telephone Number (if any)

| 5555551111 |

5. Petitioner's Email Address (if any)

| fakeclient@fakelawfirm.com |

Petitioner's Declaration and Certification

Copies of any documents I have submitted are exact photocopies of unaltered, original documents, and I understand that USCIS may require that I submit original documents to USCIS at a later date. Furthermore, I authorize the release of any information from any and all of my records that USCIS may need to determine my eligibility for the immigration benefit that I seek.

I furthermore authorize release of information contained in this petition, in supporting documents, and in my USCIS records, to other entities and persons where necessary for the administration and enforcement of U.S. immigration law.

I understand that USCIS may require me to appear for an appointment to take my biometrics (fingerprints, photograph, and/or signature) and, at that time, if I am required to provide biometrics, I will be required to sign an oath reaffirming that:

1) I reviewed and understood all of the information contained in, and submitted with, my petition; and

2) All of this information was complete, true, and correct at the time of filing.

I certify, under penalty of perjury, that all of the information in my petition and any document submitted with it were provided or authorized by me, that I reviewed and understand all of the information contained in, and submitted with my petition, and that all of this information is complete, true, and correct.

Petitioner's Signature

6.a. Petitioner's Signature

➡ | |

6.b. Date of Signature (mm/dd/yyyy) | |

NOTE TO ALL PETITIONERS: If you do not completely fill out this petition or fail to submit required documents listed in the Instructions, USCIS may deny your petition.

Part 6. Interpreter's Contact Information, Certification, and Signature

Provide the following information about the interpreter.

Interpreter's Full Name

1.a. Interpreter's Family Name (Last Name)
| |

1.b. Interpreter's Given Name (First Name)
| |

2. Interpreter's Business or Organization Name (if any)
| |

Interpreter's Mailing Address

3.a. Street Number and Name | |

3.b. ☐ Apt. ☐ Ste. ☐ Flr. | |

3.c. City or Town | |

3.d. State | | **3.e.** ZIP Code | |

3.f. Province | |

3.g. Postal Code | |

3.h. Country
| |

Part 6. Interpreter's Contact Information, Certification, and Signature (continued)

Interpreter's Contact Information

4. Interpreter's Daytime Telephone Number

5. Interpreter's Mobile Telephone Number (if any)

6. Interpreter's Email Address (if any)

Interpreter's Certification

I certify, under penalty of perjury, that:

I am fluent in English and _____,
which is the same language specified in **Part 5., Item Number 1.b.**, and I have read to this petitioner in the identified language every question and instruction on this petition and his or her answer to every question. The petitioner informed me that he or she understands every instruction, question, and answer on the petition, including the **Petitioner's Declaration and Certification,** and has verified the accuracy of every answer.

Interpreter's Signature

7.a. Interpreter's Signature

7.b. Date of Signature (mm/dd/yyyy)

Part 7. Contact Information, Declaration, and Signature of the Person Preparing this Petition, if Other Than the Petitioner

Provide the following information about the preparer.

Preparer's Full Name

1.a. Preparer's Family Name (Last Name)

Howe

1.b. Preparer's Given Name (First Name)

Barry

2. Preparer's Business or Organization Name (if any)

Dewey Cheetum and Howe Law Firm

Preparer's Mailing Address

3.a. Street Number and Name

1234 Court Street

3.b. ☐ Apt. ☐ Ste. ☐ Flr.

3.c. City or Town

Marietta

3.d. State GA   3.e. ZIP Code 30008

3.f. Province

N/A

3.g. Postal Code

N/A

3.h. Country

United States

Preparer's Contact Information

4. Preparer's Daytime Telephone Number

5555555555

5. Preparer's Mobile Telephone Number (if any)

N/A

6. Preparer's Email Address (if any)

fakelawyer@fakelawfirm.com

Preparer's Statement

7.a. ☐ I am not an attorney or accredited representative but have prepared this petition on behalf of the petitioner and with the petitioner's consent.

7.b. ☒ I am an attorney or accredited representative and my representation of the petitioner in this case ☒ extends ☐ does not extend beyond the preparation of this petition.

NOTE: If you are an attorney or accredited representative, you may need to submit a completed Form G-28, Notice of Entry of Appearance as Attorney or Accredited Representative, or Form G-28I, Notice of Entry of Appearance as Attorney In Matters Outside the Geographical Confines of the United States, with this petition.

77

Part 7. Contact Information, Declaration, and Signature of the Person Preparing this Petition, if Other Than the Petitioner (continued)

Preparer's Certification

By my signature, I certify, under penalty of perjury, that I prepared this petition at the request of the petitioner. The petitioner then reviewed this completed petition and informed me that he or she understands all of the information contained in, and submitted with, his or her petition, including the **Petitioner's Declaration and Certification**, and that all of this information is complete, true, and correct. I completed this petition based only on information that the petitioner provided to me or authorized me to obtain or use.

Preparer's Signature

8.a. Preparer's Signature

8.b. Date of Signature (mm/dd/yyyy)

78

Part 8. Additional Information

If you need extra space to provide any additional information within this petition, use the space below. If you need more space than what is provided, you may make copies of this page to complete and file with this petition or attach a separate sheet of paper. Type or print your name and A-Number (if any) at the top of each sheet; indicate the **Page Number, Part Number,** and **Item Number** to which your answer refers; and sign and date each sheet.

1.a Family Name
(Last Name)   Murphy

1.b. Given Name
(First Name)   Samuel

1.c. Middle Name

2. A-Number (if any) ▶ A-

3.a. Page Number   **3.b.** Part Number   **3.c.** Item Number

3.d.

4.a. Page Number   **4.b.** Part Number   **4.c.** Item Number

4.d.

5.a. Page Number   **5.b.** Part Number   **5.c.** Item Number

5.d.

6.a. Page Number   **6.b.** Part Number   **6.c.** Item Number

6.d.

7.a. Page Number   **7.b.** Part Number   **7.c.** Item Number

7.d.

HOW AND WHEN TO FIND A LAWYER

You are not required to have a lawyer when applying for a U.S. visa or green card. If you have a straightforward case, you may proceed successfully without a lawyer. If you are outside of the U.S., lawyers cannot attend consular interviews with you. However, they are allowed to prepare the paperwork and have follow-up communications with the consulates.

However, there are many times when a lawyer's help can make a big difference in your case and be well worth the money. Because immigration law is complicated, even a simple case can suddenly become nightmarish.

In this chapter, we'll explain:

•when applicants typically should consult an attorney

•how to find suitable counsel

•how to hire, pay, and (if necessary) fire your lawyer, and

•how to do some legal research on your own.

NOTE

If you are or have ever been, in deportation (removal) proceedings, you must see a lawyer. If the proceedings aren't yet over or are on appeal, your entire immigration situation is in the power of the courts—and you are not allowed to use most of the procedures described in this book. Even if the court proceedings are over, you should ask a lawyer whether the outcome affects your current application.

WHEN DO YOU NEED A LAWYER?

The most common legal problem encountered by would-be immigrants is the claim by USCIS or the consulate that they are inadmissible for one or more of the reasons listed, such as having spent time in the U.S. unlawfully, committed a crime, or previously lied to the U.S. government. If you know that any of these grounds apply to you, it makes sense to get legal help before you begin the application process.

Another important role for lawyers is helping explain your case to the immigration authorities. Depending on your situation, you may, for example, be trying to convince an immigration officer that you have no secret plans to stay in the U.S. permanently; are getting married for love, not for a green card; fled your country because you received verbal death threats; or are an acknowledged expert in your field. You'll be required to submit various documents to prove such things, which an attorney can help you choose and prepare.

Also, an experienced immigration attorney will often add an item that's not required—a cover letter or memo explaining what all the evidence adds up to and making clear how your case fits within the legal requirements. Written materials are difficult to produce if you are not experienced in immigration

81

law. And the lawyer may also be able to argue some of these points in person—for example, at your green card interview.

Yet another circumstance that lawyers can help with is the failure of USCIS or the consulate to act on or approve your application for reasons that have more to do with bureaucracy than law. For example, an applicant who moves from Los Angeles to San Francisco after filing a green card application might find that the application has disappeared into a bureaucratic black hole for several months. Delays at the USCIS service centers are also ridiculously common.

Lawyers don't have as much power as you—or the lawyers— might wish in such circumstances. True, the lawyer may have access to inside email inquiry lines, where they (and only they) can ask about delayed or problematic cases—but even lawyers may have trouble getting answers to such inquiries. An experienced lawyer may have contacts inside USCIS or the consulate who can give information or locate a lost file. But these lawyers can't use this privilege on an everyday basis, and long delays are truly an everyday occurrence.

The bottom line is that a lawyer in most cases has no magic words that will force the U.S. government into taking action. So, if the only help you need is by repeatedly calling or writing to USCIS or the consulate until they come up with an answer, you'll have to decide whether it's worth it to pay a lawyer for this. A very important time to hire a lawyer is if you are applying for something where you'll lose your rights if USCIS or a consulate doesn't act quickly. For example, a diversity visa lottery winner must get the immigration authorities to approve his or her green card before the supply has run out and before the end of that fiscal year, his or her chance will be lost forever. Similarly, an immigrating child about to turn 21 may, in certain circumstances, lose rights or be delayed in his or her immigration process. A good lawyer will know the latest tactics for alerting USCIS or the consulates to such issues.

SEE AN EXPERT

Don't rely on advice from USCIS information officers. Would you want the receptionist in your doctor's office to tell you whether to get brain surgery? Asking USCIS information officers for advice about your case (beyond basic procedural advice such as where to file an application and what the fees are) is equally unsafe. The people who staff USCIS phone and information services are not experts. USCIS takes no responsibility if their advice is wrong—and won't treat your application with any more sympathy. Even following the advice of officials higher up in the agency may not be safe. Always get a lawyer's opinion.

Finally, a good time to consult with an immigration lawyer is when you've researched the law and feel like you have no hope of getting a U.S. visa or green card, like reading this book. Before giving up, it's worth checking with a lawyer to make sure you haven't missed anything. This is particularly true if you have some urgent reason for needing to come to or stay in the United States—for example, you developed a serious illness while visiting the U.S. and might die if transported home. Some unusual (and hard-to-get) remedies, with names like "humanitarian parole" and "deferred action" may help

83

you. However, you'll definitely need a lawyer's assistance to apply for and obtain these remedies. We don't cover them in this book.

WHERE TO GET THE NAMES OF GOOD IMMIGRATION LAWYERS

Finding a good lawyer can involve a fair amount of work. Immigration law is a specialized area; it has many subspecialties within it. So you will want to find a lawyer who specializes in immigration—you don't want to consult the lawyer who wrote your best friend's Will.

Whatever you do, don't just open the telephone book and pick the immigration lawyer with the biggest advertisement. Ask a trusted person for a referral. Perhaps you know someone in the United States who is sophisticated in practical affairs and has been through an immigration process. This person may be able to recommend his or her lawyer or ask that lawyer to recommend another.

Also, check out Nolo's Lawyer Directory at www.nolo.com (under "Find a Lawyer," choose "Immigration Law" from the dropdown menu for Practice Area). This allows you to view lawyers' photos and personal profiles describing their areas of expertise and practice philosophy.

Local nonprofit organizations serving immigrants can also be excellent sources for low-cost services or referrals. A nonprofit organization is a charity that seeks funding from foundations and individuals to help people in need. Since they exist to serve others rather than to make a profit, they charge less and are usually staffed by people whose hearts and minds are in the right places. In the immigrant services field, examples include Northwest Immigrant Rights Project (Seattle), El Rescate (Los Angeles), the various International Institutes (nationwide), and Catholic Charities (nationwide).

For a list of U.S. government-approved nonprofits and attorneys who'll work for reduced fees, ask your local USCIS office or court or check www.justice.gov/eoir (click "Find Legal Representation" in the Action Center, then "List of Pro Bono Legal Service Providers"). You don't need to use a nonprofit from this list, but it may be safer. Supposed nonprofit organizations can be unscrupulous too, or they may be for-profit businesses. Most nonprofits keep lists of lawyers who they know do honest immigration work for a fair price.

Yet another good resource is the American Immigration Lawyers Association (AILA)—at 202-507-7600 or www.aila.org. AILA offers a lawyer referral service. Its membership is limited to lawyers who have passed a screening process, which helps keep out the less-scrupulous practitioners. But not all good immigration lawyers have joined AILA (membership is a bit pricey and for the elite few).

Try to get a list of a few lawyers you've heard do good work, then meet or talk to each and choose one. If you're living in another country now, you may have to communicate with a U.S.-based lawyer primarily by email. In major cities of some countries with high levels of immigration, such as Canada and England, U.S. immigration firms have set up offices.

NOTE

Don't contact lawyers expecting free advice. Good immigration lawyers are extremely busy and under a lot of deadline pressure. Yet many receive supposed "quick questions," particularly via email, from people who are not their clients and whom they've never met. It's unfair to expect a response and unrealistic to assume that you'll get valid advice without a full analysis of your situation.

HOW TO AVOID SLEAZY LAWYERS

There are good and bad immigration lawyers out there. Some of the good ones are candidates for sainthood—they put in long hours dealing with a difficult bureaucracy on behalf of a clientele that typically can't pay high fees. They are also active in the community, advocating for immigrants' rights when no one else does.

The bad immigration lawyers are a nightmare—and more than a few are out there. They typically try to do a high-volume business, churning out the same forms for every client regardless of their situation. Such lawyers (if they're lawyers at all) can get clients into deep trouble by overlooking critical issues in their cases or failing to submit applications or court materials on time. But they never seem to forget to charge for their supposed help. Some signs to watch for are:

86

- ✓ The lawyer approaches you in a USCIS office or another public location and tries to solicit your business. This is not only against the lawyers' rules of professional ethics but also indicates that the lawyer may be incompetent—no good lawyer ever needs to find clients this way.
- ✓ The lawyer makes big promises, such as "I guarantee I'll win your case" or "I've got a special contact who will put your application at the front of the line." The U.S. government is in ultimate control of your application, and any lawyer who implies that he or she has special powers is either lying or may be involved in something you don't want to be a part of.
- ✓ The lawyer has a fancy office and wears a lot of flashy gold jewelry. We're all for a professional appearance, but a fancy office or a $2,000 outfit aren't necessarily signs of a lawyer's success at winning cases. These trappings may be signs that the lawyer charges high fees and counts on impressing clients with clothing rather than results.
- ✓ The lawyer encourages you to lie on your application. This is a tricky area. On the one hand, a good lawyer can assist you in learning what information you don't want to needlessly offer up and can help you present the truth in the best light possible. But a lawyer who coaches you to lie—for example, by telling you to pretend you lost your passport and visa when you entered the United States illegally—isn't ethical. There's every chance that USCIS knows the lawyer's reputation and will scrutinize your application harder.

You might think the really bad lawyers would be out of business by now, but that isn't the case. Sadly, neither the attorney bar associations nor the courts, nor even the police takes much interest in going after people who prey on immigrants. Occasionally, nonprofits devoted to immigrants' rights will attempt to get the enforcement community interested in taking action. Unfortunately, this threat of official scrutiny isn't much of a deterrent.

T.I.P.

If you are the victim of an unscrupulous lawyer, complain! Law enforcement won't go after lawyers who prey on immigrants until there is enough community pressure. If a lawyer, or someone pretending to be a lawyer, pulls something unethical on you, report it to the state and local bar association and the local district attorney's (DA's) office. Ask your local nonprofits if anyone else in your area is collecting such information.

HOW TO CHOOSE AMONG LAWYERS

Once you've got your "short list" of prospective lawyers, you'll want to speak to each. How much a lawyer charge is bound to be a factor in whom you choose, but it shouldn't be the only factor. Here are some other important considerations.

1. Familiarity With Cases Like Yours

Some immigration lawyers spend much of their time in subspecialties, such as helping people obtain asylum or employment-based visas. To learn how much experience a lawyer has in the type of visa or green card you're interested in, ask practical questions, such as:

- ✓ How long do you expect my case to take?
- ✓ What is the reputation of the USCIS or consular office officers who will handle my case?
- ✓ How many cases like mine did you handle this year?

2. Client Rapport

Your first instinct in hiring a lawyer may be to look for a shark— someone you wouldn't want to leave your child with but who will be a tough fighter for your case. This isn't necessarily the best choice in the immigration context. Since you may need to discuss highly confidential issues with your lawyer, you'll want to know that the person is discreet and thoughtful. Also, realize that a lawyer's politeness goes a long way in front of immigration officials; sharks often produce a bureaucratic backlash, whereas lawyers with good working relations with USCIS may have doors opened to them.

3. Access to Your Lawyer

You'll want to know that you can reach your lawyer during the months that your application winds its way through the USCIS or consular bureaucracy. A lawyer's accessibility may be hard to judge initially, but try listening to the receptionist as you wait in the lawyer's office for the first time. If you get the sense that the receptionist is rude and trying to push people off or give flimsy excuses about why the lawyer hasn't returned their calls or won't talk to them, don't hire that lawyer.

Many immigration lawyers are sole practitioners and use voicemail rather than a receptionist. In that case, you'll have to rely on how quickly they answer your initial calls. In your first meeting, ask the lawyer how quickly he or she will get back to you. If the lawyer regularly breaks promises, you'll have grounds on which to complain.

Of course, you, too, have a responsibility not to harass your lawyer with frequent calls. The lawyer should be available for legitimate questions about your case, including inquiries about approaching deadlines.

4. Explaining Services and Costs

Look at any printed materials the lawyer gives you on your first visit. Are they glitzy, glossy pieces that look more like advertising than useful? Or are they designed to acquaint you with the process you're getting into and the lawyer's role in it? Think about this issue again before you sign the lawyer's fee agreement described in the section immediately below. Being a good salesperson doesn't necessarily make someone a good lawyer.

SIGNING UP YOUR LAWYER

Many good lawyers will ask you to sign an agreement covering their services and the fees you will pay them. This is a good idea for both of you and can help prevent misunderstandings. The contract should be written in a way you can understand; there's no law that says it has to be in confusing legal jargon. The lawyer should go over the contract with you carefully, not just push it under your nose, saying, "Sign here." Some normal contract clauses include:

- ✓ Scope of work. A description of exactly what the lawyer will do for you.
- ✓ Fees. Specification of the amount you'll pay, either as a flat fee (a lump sum you pay for a stated task, such as $2,000 for an adjustment of status application) or at an hourly rate, with a payment schedule. If you hire someone at an hourly rate, you can ask to be told as soon as the hours have hit a certain limit.

- ✓ Responsibility for expenses. Most lawyers will ask you to cover incidental expenses associated with your cases, such as phone calls, postage, and photocopying. This is fair. After all, if your case requires a one-hour phone call to the consulate in Brunei, that call shouldn't eat up the lawyer's fee. But check carefully to be sure that the lawyer charges you the actual costs of these items. Some lawyers have been known to turn a tidy profit by charging, for example, 20 cents a page for a photocopy job that cost only three cents a page.

- ✓ Effect of nonpayment. Many lawyers charge interest if you fail to pay on time. This is normal and probably not worth making a big fuss about. If you have trouble paying on time, call the lawyer and ask for more time—he or she may be willing to forgo the interest if it's clear you're taking your obligation seriously.
- ✓ Exclusion of guarantee. The lawyer may warn you that there's no guarantee of winning your case. Though this may appear as if the lawyer is looking for an excuse to lose, it is actually a responsible way for the lawyer to protect against clients who assume they're guaranteed a win or who later accuse the lawyer of having made such promises. After all, USCIS or the consulate is the ultimate decision-maker on your case.

Watch Out for Nonlawyers Practicing

Immigration Law

Because much immigration law involves filling in forms, people assume it's easy. They're wrong. Be careful about whom you consult with or hand your case over to. Unless the person shows you certification that he or she is a lawyer, an accredited representative, or a paralegal working under the direct supervision of a lawyer, think of them as typists. (An accredited representative is a nonlawyer who has received training from a lawyer and been recognized

92

by USCIS as qualified to prepare USCIS applications and represent clients in court.)

This is true even for people who go by fancy names such as "immigration consultant," "notario," or "notary public" – they do not have a law degree. To check on whether someone is a lawyer, ask for his or her bar number and call the state bar association.

Hiring a nonlawyer or nonaccredited representative is appropriate only if you want help with the form preparation and no more. But even seemingly minor details asked for on a form, like your date of entry to the U. S. or your address, can have legal consequences. Don't just turn your case over and let the consultant make the decisions.

If you feel an immigration consultant has defrauded you, you may want to sue in small claims court; see Everybody's Guide to Small Claims Court by Cara O'Neill (Nolo).

✓ Effect of changes in the case. Most lawyers will warn you that if there is something you didn't tell them about (for example, that you are still married to your first wife while trying to get a green card through your second wife) or a significant life change affects your case (for instance, you get arrested), they will charge you additional fees to cover the added work these revelations will cause. This, too, is normal; but to prevent disputes, make very sure that the contract specifies in detail all the work that is already included. For example, a contract for a lawyer to help you with a green card application within the United States might specify that the lawyer will be responsible for "preparation of visa petition and adjustment of status packet, filing all applications with USCIS, representation at an interview, and reasonable follow-up with USCIS." If the lawyer agrees to include work on any special waivers or unusual documents (for example, waiver of inadmissibility or an extra Affidavit of Support from a joint sponsor), make sure these are mentioned in the contract.

PAYING YOUR LAWYER

You may have to pay an initial consultation fee as well as a fee for the lawyer's services. The initial consultation fee can vary depending on the lawyer and your case but usually is no less than $100. Some lawyers will treat the initial consultation fee as part payment for full services if you hire them.

Some good lawyers provide free consultations. But many have found that they can't afford to spend a lot of their time this way since many immigrants have no visa or remedy available, so the lawyer gets no work after the initial consultation. Be ready to pay a reasonable fee for your initial consultation, but do not sign any contracts for further services until you're confident you've found the right lawyer. This usually means consulting several lawyers before signing a contract with the one you like best.

Many lawyers charge flat rates for green card applications. That means you can compare prices. If the lawyer quotes an hourly rate, expect to pay between $150 and $350 per hour.

A higher rate doesn't necessarily mean a better lawyer. Those who charge less may be keeping their overhead low, making their name in the business, or philosophically opposed to charging high fees. But an extremely low fee may be a sign that the person isn't a lawyer, as covered in "Watch Out for Nonlawyers Practicing Immigration Law" above.

If the prices you are being quoted are beyond your reach, but you need legal help, you have a couple of options. One is to ask the lawyer to split the work with you. With this arrangement, the lawyer consults with you solely about the issue causing you difficulty, reviews a document, or performs some other key task at the hourly rate while you do the follow-up work, such as filling out the application forms and translating or writing documents, statements, letters, or more.

Be forewarned, though, that while many lawyers will sell you advice on an hourly basis, most won't want to get into a mixed arrangement unless they are sure they won't end up cleaning up anything you might do wrong. For example, a lawyer might not agree to represent you in a USCIS interview if the lawyer wasn't hired to review your forms and documents before submitting them to USCIS.

Another option is to look for a nonprofit organization that helps people with cases like yours. A few provide free services, while most charges reduced rates. But don't get your hopes too high. The U.S. government does not fund organizations that provide services to immigrants (except for very limited types of services), which means that most nonprofits depend on private sources of income and are chronically underfunded. The result is that many nonprofits will have long backlogs of cases and may not be able to take your case at all.

FIRING YOUR LAWYER

You have the right to fire your lawyer at any time. But before you take this step, make sure your disagreement is about something that is truly the lawyer's fault.

Many people blame their lawyer for delays that are caused by USCIS or the consulates. You can always consult with another lawyer regarding whether your case has been mishandled. Ask your lawyer for a complete copy of your file; you have a right to your file at any time. If it appears that your case was mishandled, or if relations with your lawyer have deteriorated badly, firing the lawyer may be the healthiest thing for you and your immigration case.

You will have to pay the fired lawyer for any work that has already been done on your case. If you paid any money upfront before the work was done, the lawyer probably was required to put it in a trust account, which is a special bank account where the money doesn't legally belong to the lawyer until he or she does the required work. When the lawyer-client relationship ends, the lawyer is permitted to withdraw enough money from the trust account to cover the work already done. If you had a flat-fee arrangement, the lawyer calculates how much he or she is due using a percentage or hourly rate, limited by the total flat-fee amount. Ask for a complete accounting of how the lawyer decided how much to keep. Don't count on getting any money back, however—flat fees are often artificially low, and it's very easy for a lawyer to show that he or she used up your fee on the work that was done.

Firing your lawyer will not affect the progress of your applications with USCIS or the consulate. However, you should send a letter to the last USCIS or consular office you heard from, directing them to send all future correspondence directly to you (or your new lawyer).

DO-IT-YOURSELF LEGAL RESEARCH

With or without a lawyer, you may at some point wish to look at the immigration laws yourself. If so, we applaud your self-empowerment instinct—but need to give you a few warnings. A government spokesperson once called the immigration laws a "mystery, and a mastery of obfuscation" (spokeswoman Karen Kraushaar, quoted in The Washington Post, April 24, 2001). They've only gotten worse since she said that. One is tempted to think that the members of the U.S. Congress who write and amend the immigration laws deliberately made them unreadable, perhaps to confuse the rest of the representatives so they wouldn't understand what they were voting on.

The result is that researching the immigration laws is something even the experts find difficult—which means you may be wading into treacherous waters if you try it on your own. Figuring out local USCIS office procedures and policies can be even more difficult. Lawyers learn a great deal through trial and error and the experiences of other lawyers who tried new tactics. They also learn important information from USCIS or State Department cables, memos, or other instructions, which can sometimes be found online but you have to know what you're looking for.

Does all this mean that you shouldn't ever do your own legal research? Certainly not. Some research inquiries are quite safe—for instance, if we've cited a section of the law and you want to read the exact language or see whether that section has changed, there's no magic in looking up the law and reading it. But generally, be cautious when researching, and look at several sources to confirm your findings.

Immigration laws are federal, meaning they are written by the U.S. Congress and do not vary from one state to another (though procedures and priorities for interpreting and carrying out the laws may vary among USCIS offices in different cities, states, or federal court circuits). Below we give you a rundown on the most accessible research tools. Not coincidentally, lawyers often use these tools as well.

1. The Federal Code

The federal immigration law is in Title 8 of the United States Code. Any law library (such as the one at your local courthouse or law school) should have a complete set of the U.S. Code (traditionally abbreviated as U.S.C.). The library may also have a separate volume containing the same material, called the Immigration and Nationality Act, or I.N.A.

Unfortunately, the two sets of laws are numbered a bit differently, and not all volumes of the I.N.A. cross-reference back to the U.S. Code and vice versa. You can also access the I.N.A. at www.uscis.gov, under the "Legal Resources" tab.

2. USCIS and State Department Regulations and Guidance

Another important source of immigration law is the Code of Federal Regulations (C.F.R.). Federal regulations are written by the agencies responsible for carrying out federal law. The regulations are meant to explain in greater detail just how the federal agency will carry out the law. You'll find the USCIS regulations at Title 8 of the C.F.R.; the Department of State regulations (relevant to anyone whose application is being decided at a U.S. consulate) at Title 22 of the C.F.R.; and the Department of Labor regulations at 20 C.F.R.

If you are applying to USCIS for immigration status or benefit, the USCIS Policy Manual (www.uscis.gov/policymanual/HTML/PolicyManual.html) is a great resource understanding how USCIS will look at your case. (The Policy Manual is replacing, piece by piece, the USCIS Adjudicator's Field Manual.)

The regulations are helpful but certainly don't have all the answers.

Again, your local law library will have the C.F.R., as will uscis.gov.

If you are applying for a visa from outside of the U.S., you may also wish to look at the State Department's Foreign Affairs Manual. This is primarily meant to be an internal government document containing instructions to the consulates on handling immigrant and nonimmigrant visa cases. However, it is available for public research as well. See https://fam.state.gov.

3. Online Information

You will want to familiarize yourself with the USCIS, State Department, and Labor Department websites. The addresses are www.uscis.gov, www.travel.state.gov, and www.doleta.gov (for the Labor Department's Employment & Training Administration).

The USCIS website offers brief advice on various immigration benefits and applications, downloads of most immigration forms, and current fees.

Much of the useful information on the State Department website is found under "U.S. Visas."

The Department of Labor website, www.foreignlaborcert.doleta.gov, contains programs for hiring foreign workers, application forms, F.A.Q.s, and more.

The Internet is full of sites put up by immigration lawyers as well as immigrants. Because the quality of these sites varies widely, we don't even attempt to review them here.

4. Court Decisions

Immigrants denied visas or green cards often appeal these decisions to the federal courts. The courts' decisions in these cases should govern the future behavior of USCIS and the consulates.

However, you should hardly ever need to discuss court decisions with a USCIS or State Department official. For one thing, the officials are not likely to listen until they get a specific directive from their superiors or until the court decision is incorporated into their agency's regulations (the C.F.R.). For another thing, such discussions probably mean that your case has become complicated enough to need a lawyer. We do not attempt to teach you how to research federal court decisions here.

FREQUENTLY ASKED QUESTIONS

Q. What is the process for extending a visa beyond the original four-month validity?

A. The process is very simple. A consular officer can revalidate a K visa petition any number of times for additional periods of 4 months, provided the officer concludes that the petitioner and beneficiary remain legally free to marry and continue to intend to marry each other within 90 days after the beneficiary's admission into the United States. To have the petition revalidated mail or fax a written request to the Embassy that includes a statement of your intention to go forward with the marriage.

Q. Do dependent children receiving K-2 visas need to travel to the United States at the same time as the K-1 beneficiary?

A. No, eligible dependent children can travel to the United States on a K-2 visa within a year of the issuance of the K-1 visa to the principal beneficiary. This is true even if the K-1 beneficiary has subsequently married, provided the dependent child is still unmarried and under 21 years of age at the time of K-2 issuance. If a dependent child of your fiancé seeks to enter the United States more than one year after your fiancé has received a K-1 visa, it will be necessary to file an immigrant visa petition for the child.

Q. Should I include all of my fiancé's children in the K visa petition?

A. USCIS holds that all children of a K-1 beneficiary must be listed on the visa petition. If the beneficiary has a child not named in the petition, the consular officer must suspend action and return the petition to USCIS for reconsideration.

Q. What if my fiancé is pregnant and this is not disclosed on the approved petition?

A. Visa processing can continue in this case if the consular officer obtains a statement indicating awareness of the pregnancy and the desire to proceed with the marriage.

Q. If I decide not to get married to my fiancé can I cancel the petition?

A. You should make a written request to the Embassy asking to withdraw the petition. You may wish to notarize such a statement so we can be assured that you personally are asking the petition to be withdrawn.

Q. If my fiancé entered the U.S. on a K visa but had to leave before we were married, what can I do to get my fiancé a new K visa?

A. K visas are issued valid for a single entry and a 6-month period. If a beneficiary has returned abroad prior to the marriage, the consular officer may issue a new K visa provided that the period of validity does not exceed the 90th day after the date of initial admission of the alien on the original K visa and also provided that the petitioner and beneficiary still intend and are free to marry. After the 90th day, unless other arrangements have been made with USCIS prior to your fiancé's departure, you will need to start the K visa process again.

FOR MORE INFORMATION, CONSULTANT, AND
LEGAL ADVICE, VISIT

Shaw 3 Law Firm *@ www.shaw3lawfirm.com*